HEART LIGHT

Rescue at Sea

A True Story

by Diviana

*T*his *B*ook is *D*edicated

To my husband Darryl whose breakthrough and heart made it possible for us to be here to share this experience with you.

To my son Shane for his courage.

To my mother for her perseverance.

To Captain Bruce White for 'being there'.

And the total sum of all appreciation to the BRIH.

Random House New Zealand Ltd
(An imprint of the Random House Group)

18 Poland Road
Glenfield
Auckland 10
NEW ZEALAND

Associated companies, branches and representatives throughout the world.

First published in 1995
© Diviana and Darryl Wheeler 1995
ISBN 1 86941 256 7
Printed by GP Print in New Zealand

Cover illustration by Shaun Campbell.

All rights reserved. No part of this publication may be reproduced or transmitted in any form or by any means, electronic or mechanical, including photocopying, recording, storage in any information retrieval system or otherwise, without the written permission of the publisher.

Contents

1	Tear in the Fabric	1
2	The Briefing	6
3	*Heart Light*	13
4	Just call me Storm	29
5	Destiny or Fate?	37
6	All is Well — All is at Peace	46
7	A Break in Third-dimensional Reality	54
8	War in Heaven — Hell on the High Seas	74
9	The Kingdom of Heaven is Near at Hand	90
10	Tear in the Fabric	106
11	In the Eye of the Vortex	113
12	The *San Te Maru 18*	124
13	Rescue at Sea	141
14	Cauac: The Omega	159
15	Ahua: The Alpha	168

Appendix
A Safe Cruising Guide for Catamarans
by Darryl Wheeler — 185

Epilogue — 196

Thanks to

PAUL CAMPBELL, who after 20 years of pragmatic international television reporting, allowed his own 'magical child' within to come forward and add its own special flavour of elixir to this manuscript.

JACHEME PILAR and VOUDRIN XN DARRAH, whose years of teaching children made sure all the 'Is' were dotted and all the 'Ts' were crossed.

ELIZABETH and ALLAN YORK who selflessly offered their home and resources so that our healing could take place.

A special thank you to DAVID BALDOCK at Ninox Films for his unselfish and generous sharing of information after endless interviews with storm victims and rescuers for his documentary, *Rescue South Pacific*, to be released internationally in 1995.

The cover illustration is an actual photograph of *Heart Light* scanned into artwork of the storm.

Chapter 1

Tear in the Fabric

As if in a surrealistic dream, I could hear the shrill sound of the seas exploding like bombs as they crashed down upon our 42-foot catamaran *Heart Light*. Winds gusting over 90 knots were blowing the tops off the immense waves, making us a target for these massive missiles. Over 20,000 pounds of water was being hurled down upon us at 65 to 70 knots, slamming down on to the yacht with such force that the cabin structure and windows were flexing, pouring gallons of water into our fragile refuge.

Throughout the previous days and nights the airwaves of our single side-band radio had been filled with astonished seafarers unable to make sense of the sudden and unexpected phenomenon taking place over 500 miles from the nearest landfall. We had been listening to traumatic calls for help from distressed yachts, many of them participating in the Tongan Regatta Race outward bound from Auckland, New Zealand. We knew there were people in distress, being pitch-poled, capsizing and possibly dying all around us in the maelstrom. I felt so much love for *Heart Light*, for she had taken on a life of her own. For hours, she had been fighting valiantly to keep us safe and alive during this violent, seemingly endless, storm.

At the best of times, the seas were averaging 50 feet in height. But as the storm shrieked, winds of 75 to 80 knots were gusting up to 90 knots, driving the mammoth waves on top of one another, and stacking them, at times, to an unbelievable 100 feet high. Whenever we caught one of these giants, our big catamaran lurched and became airborne until she could find her grip and once again slip-slide down the massive seas.

I looked up at my love as he fought exhaustion after hours of constantly focusing on keeping *Heart Light* surfing and upright. Since there was no harness at the indoor steering station, I was holding Darryl down in his captain's seat. The hulls were rising so high, with enormous velocity and without warning, that it was impossible for him to stay in his seat. I had wrapped my body, embryo-shaped, around him and was massaging him with my free hand, giving him words of support to keep him awake.

Before we had sailed I had warned him of danger, so he had kept checking the weather reports. Keri Keri radio, on the east coast of New Zealand's North Island, had been given and were giving glowing reports of balmy weather. Only hours before the storm struck, the radio operator had expressed hopes that everyone had enough fuel on board as the winds were likely to dwindle and motoring might become necessary. Even so, Darryl had not been able to sleep well since the beginning of the voyage. He knew in his heart that I had not yet been wrong in one of my extrasensory predictions.

Suddenly, our first serious broach. I was thrown across the yacht. The first impact I felt was hitting the wall; the second was Darryl's full weight slamming into me. Never before have I ever seen so much pure adrenalin in action, as Darryl scrambled for the wheel to bring *Heart Light* back under control.

I wasn't moving so fast, my body racked with pain. I didn't know the extent of my injuries and so chose to take time to find out. Shane, our 29-year-old son, had superior weight and strength, and so took over as guardian of the helmsman. As I looked at Shane, my eyes filled with a new vision, not of a son, but of an emerging brother. His courage and willingness to do whatever was asked of him had filled my heart with respect and appreciation.

In the end, Shane would spend over nine straight hours holding his father in the captain's seat. Like a football linebacker, he had pressed his shoulders into his father's, wrapped his arms around him and ignored his own persistent discomfort. Despite our peril, I found a fleeting moment to tease them mischievously, 'I haven't seen you two boys get this close in years!'

Since the onset of the storm, I had been in a meditative semi-altered state of consciousness. I had been listening and storing information being given to me through a myriad of audible inter-dimensional voices as we drew closer and closer to the centre of the foretold vortex and the impending event. I had been forewarned that a tear in the fabric of third-dimensional reality would create a war in the heavens, and hell on the high seas. As the forces of light and dark clashed, human fate was being sealed, one way or the other, forever.

Bringing more of my consciousness into my body, I peered through the dark at my daughter-in-law, Shali, sitting on the floor holding herself down against the violent movements of the yacht. It was now 4.30 am on Sunday morning. For some time Shali had been vomiting blood from relentless seasickness. During one perilous point in the storm, she had been thrown brutally from her bunk and deeply bruised. I felt that she had gone into a passive state of shock. She was very quiet, very stout hearted.

As the savage storm raged on I knew the end was very near. It was time to prepare everyone for their possible physical departure from this world. I called out to them, 'Shane, Shali, come over here please.' They joined me on the floor next to the indoor steering station. Above us, Darryl clung to the wheel, where only the faint glow of the instruments illuminated his face. 'Darryl, can you hear me?' I asked. He looked down, his eyes full of love and a calm surrendered peace, and replied almost in a whisper, 'Yes'.

'We are very close to the centre of the vortex now,' I began. 'It is not yet known whether we are going to take our physical departure there or not. In case we do have to leave, we must prepare ourselves. Now listen carefully to what I am about to tell you. When you were born into this world, you were in your mother's womb, which was filled with salt water. You were safe, cradled, and loved in that environment. Your bodies have that memory stored in them. The minute you release your clinging to them they will immediately go into a state of joy, not fear.

'You have been taught you are not your bodies; you can feel the truth can't you?' I asked as I watched them nod their heads attentively. 'For us to leave our bodies in peace we must focus on this truth. If necessary, together, we will release them in joy.'

I looked at Shane and directed him, 'If the boat starts to go down, it will be your job to open the door, do you understand?'

'Yes, Mother,' he replied.

I knew that if they were caught like rats in a trap, with

the boat upside down, no way out, and filling with water they might lose their centres and panic. I felt that, if they were kept moving, their minds wouldn't get caught up in fear and they would have a smoother transition.

Tenderly, I continued, 'Then you will all follow me outside back into mother's womb. We will all go swimming, all of us together.'

'And the water's pretty warm where we are now,' quipped Shane.

We all laughed and Shali said, 'Good, I don't like swimming in cold water!'

At that moment everything went into slow motion as Darryl was thrown violently from the captain's chair. The hull lifted higher and higher and, with an ear-shattering sound, we heard *Heart Light* roar her final death screams as she careened down a 100-foot wave out of control. It felt like she was being hit from all sides by a freight train.

Still in slow motion — up, up, up she went — 80, 85, 90 degrees, until she was standing straight up with one hull flying through the air. We were thrown on to the cabin wall, which had now become the floor. Darryl and I knew that once *Heart Light* was at 95 degrees, her mast would be under the water and the momentum and weight of mast and halyards would carry her over.

I looked at Shane. His hand went for the door as he screamed, 'GOD NOOOOO!'

CHAPTER 2

The Briefing

This is the astonishing true story of how, together, the yacht *Heart Light* and her crew fought a battle against forces as yet on the edge of human understanding.

On Tuesday 30 May 1994, *Heart Light*, along with the last of the Tongan Cruising Regatta fleet, left New Zealand in ideal sailing conditions with the blessings of all South Pacific weather stations. However, despite excellent forecasts, state-of-the-art technology and satellites, within 72 hours perfect cruising weather became a force 12 storm and an international disaster. A storm appeared abruptly some 540 miles northeast of New Zealand, and 500 miles south of Fiji and Tonga, on Friday 3 June.

From out of nowhere came a nameless nightmare, a supernatural storm that would rampage for four days. What was more extraordinary was the fact that at its height the tempest would stay at a mindless level of ferocity for over 36 hours. That, along with the experiences of those people caught up in the storm, make it one of the greatest phenomena of this century.

Some survivors reported seeing strange and terrifying phenomena as the elements raged. Many reported hearing foreign-sounding voices, speaking in high-pitched tones, all around them. Even regatta yachts on the fringe, miles from the centre of the storm, reported hearing bizarre voices coming from the void. Others reported seeing holographic apparitions, while the crew of one yacht reported what they could only describe as a meteor flashing past them. Yet others logged mysterious green, white and orange bright objects flying through the air and lighting up the heavens. Subsequent air force investigations found that there were no ships or yachts in the vicinity to claim responsibility for these lights.

The crew of the yacht *Ramtha* have told how their decks suddenly lit up as bright as day as they lay helplessly hove to during the height of the storm. Roughly 300 feet above them was a 'huge, luminous green sphere' that slowly turned to white with tinges of orange as they watched incredulously. *Ramtha*'s skipper, a retired commercial pilot, later stated: 'I've seen a lot of lightning because I fly and I see all different types of lightning — the whole works — and at close hand. But this was nothing like lightning.'

Also caught up in the drama was Andrew Saunderson from the Royal New Zealand naval survey ship *Monowai*. 'At approximately 4 am, Sunday June 5, we saw a mysterious green light — turning to white light — that flashed and lit up the sky. It had been too large and bright to have been a flare of any kind.' His watch mate added: 'We could see for miles. It was really quite strange.' The massive light hovered above their vessel for quite some time before disappearing into the storm.

Don Mundell, the Tongan Regatta coordinator, has written: 'The rapid increase in wind strength whipped the sea into a frenzy. The storm system was moving so fast that it roared down on unsuspecting yachts sailing to Fiji and Tonga. As a consequence, around 30 yachts and at least 100 lives were threatened.' Rescuing those in danger was an international effort, involving the cargo vessels *Tui Cakau* and the *Nordic Duchess*, the fishing vessel *San Te Maru 18*, the French naval ship *Jacques Cartier* and the New Zealand naval ship the *Monowai*.

Fourteen Emergency Position Indicating Radio Beacons (EPIRB) were set off. Six yachts were rolled. Five yachts were dismasted. One yacht was pitch-poled, rolled and dismasted. (Pitch-poling is when a yacht nose-dives off the top of a wave into the water below, usually to the bottom of the sea.) By the time the seas had calmed, many yachts had been lost and 21 people had been rescued. Three people had drowned.

To fully understand the magnitude of this storm, we can compare it to the 1979 storm that struck the Fastnet Yacht Race 70 miles off the English coast. Quoted as the worst disaster in 100 years of ocean yacht racing, this 'mother of all storms' created bedlam for over 14 hours. It was a full force 10 storm, with seas reaching 50 feet.

Well-known yachting enthusiast, Ted Turner, has stated: 'It was the roughest race in the history of ocean racing. I've sailed over 100,000 miles off shore in some of the toughest races around the world — a number of transatlantic races — and I've never seen the likes of the conditions encountered in this Fastnet.' Rescue operations, involving the British Royal Navy and the Royal Air Force, and cargo and fishing vessels, have become the stuff of maritime legends.

Rather than a comparison of tragedies, this is a comparison between the force and velocity of the Fastnet storm and the anonymous horror that swept the Pacific over Queen's Birthday Weekend 1994. The largest air and sea rescue search in the history of New Zealand started on Saturday 4 June, but the rescue coordination centre in Wellington could do little more than *monitor the havoc*.

Winds gusting 90 knots and massive seas beat back the ships brave enough to try to reach those in distress. For a time the 3400-ton *Monowai* was unable to help yachts just south of her position, because she found herself in danger and was forced to run on a westerly heading till conditions eased. Commander Larry Robins has stated that the *Monowai* rolled frightfully, up to 48 degrees, in the monstrous seas as he and his crew stood 'white knuckled' on watch.

The conditions were too tumultuous for anyone to get into a life-raft. When the *Monowai* was finally able to reach some of the survivors, lifelines with rescue harnesses attached were fired over to the yacht. *Monowai*'s crew then dragged the waterlogged survivors back through 300 feet or more of frothing sea before lifting them up by crane to safety.

The *San Te Maru 18*, a 364-ton fishing vessel, was asked to assist in the rescue of three boats, but her crew also found themselves in peril and were forced to run for their lives as the storm took them many miles off course. Captain Bruce White of the *San Te Maru 18* later stated: 'I have been fishing over 20 years in these waters and off the Tasman. I have been in force 10 storms, but I have never seen seas the likes of this storm, ever!'

Above the tempest, frustrations built as emergency-beacon signals and distress calls crackled into the receivers on the Royal New Zealand Air Force Orion circling helplessly high overhead. Flight Lieutenant Bruce Craies, who has logged over 4000 flying hours, stated he had never seen conditions as bad anywhere. 'If there was a force 12 on the scale, that is what it would have been.

Wing Commander Craig Inch of the RNZAF Orion crew has told how, at an altitude of 6000 to 7000 feet, he and his crew were in balmy blue skies and 15-knot winds.

Then, when they reached the coordinates for the first beacon locator signal and dove down through the clouds below: 'All hell broke loose. It was as if a bomb went off as we descended down to about 2000 feet above sea-level.' In less than a minute they had gone from 15 to 80 knots of wind!

'It was totally diabolical. We couldn't believe it. We were measuring towering waves up to 100 feet in height.' Their radar had become useless, and at times they found themselves torn between flying through the cloud cover to safety or boldly staying to keep watch on the besieged yachts. Although some of the crew became unmercifully motion sick in the relentless turbulence, the Orion valiantly remained above their vulnerable charges.

Paul Everett, a crew member on the yacht *Irresistible*, which was on its way to Fiji, later wrote: 'How big is a wave if a 51-foot yacht is halfway down, with 50 feet behind it and 50 feet still to go before it reaches the bottom?' The skipper of another yacht, *Swanhaven*, has stated: 'The barometer dropped a total 42 points in less than 36 hours — 14 points in 12 hours. The waves were huge; most were breaking. I couldn't look into the wind — it was like gravel being thrown into my face.'

There has been much speculation on how this storm started. The New Zealand Meteorological Service has speculated that the unusual conditions were caused by 'low index weather'. It is calling the storm 'an extreme example of a squash zone — a bomb'. Conditions were almost perfect when the yachts left New Zealand. It looked like nothing could go wrong. The Met Service states that a tropical depression began forming between Vanuatu and Fiji on Friday 3 June. Even after the system reached its highest intensity, with a central pressure of around 979 hPa, it was slow to both move off and decay, a fact that *Heart Light* was only too well aware of at the time.

Conflicting evidence of the storm's path comes from the yacht *Sofia*, which was sailing northeast towards Tonga. She reported a 'strange encounter', *early* on Friday morning, with a large freighter, about 240 feet long, that didn't appear to be named and that refused to identify itself.

According to *Sofia*'s skipper, 'They came across our bow about 300 feet away going from east to west. We contacted them on the VHF radio and they said there was a force 12 storm *northeast* of us. They'd been in 50-foot seas and told us to get the hell out of there.'

That report conflicts with the Met Service report in two significant ways — time and direction. *Sofia* was warned of the storm *early* on the Friday morning, whereas the Met Service states that the depression *started to form* on Friday 3 June. The ship the *Sofia* encountered was sailing west and had *come through* a storm. However, the Met Service has stated that the storm began between Vanuatu and Fiji, to the *northwest* of *Sofia*, and then moved south at approximately 500 miles a day.

Asked if he could help clarify this mystery, *Sofia*'s skipper replied: 'It could possibly be human error.' Asked if it could be his error, he promptly asserted: 'I know which way we were going and I know which way that ship was going.' His crew verify this.

Don Mundell has stated: 'This time of year above 30 degrees latitude you expect it to be pretty fine. However, this storm had been very, very vicious at the 30 degree zone.'

One of two people aboard *Destiny*, one of the first yachts to start feeling the effects of the storm, has been reported as saying: 'Unbelievably, the wind rose again. We were both feeling real concern and so we decided to issue a Pan emergency call on the HF radio to alert authorities both to our circumstances and to the ferocity of the storm — a fact not known to meteorologists at the time.'

Was the storm in the South Pacific over Queen's Birthday Weekend 1994 a freak accident of nature? Or was it a tempest caused by forces we are only just learning about? You choose as you read the rest of this book.

Chapter 3

*H*eart *L*ight

9 May 1988
■ 7:00 pm ■

Sailing the vast expanse of blue had never really been an ambition of either Darryl or myself, though what began as a chance encounter was to change all that.

Darryl and I were sitting chatting over the bustling background noise from the cheerful happy-hour crowd at the St Petersburg Elks Club in Florida when we were interrupted by an energetic voice. 'Hey, who owns that monster bus parked across the street?' a man was asking the bartender. Before the bartender could reply, Darryl, sitting next to the standing stranger, responded with pride, 'We do'.

Looking out the window, I realized it had become dark outside, and the computer had switched on the night lights around our 40-foot touring bus. The lights shone like little twinkling Christmas-tree lights, lending the big coach an impressive, and slightly surrealistic, appearance.

Six months earlier my book, *The Great Awakening*, had been published, and Darryl and I were on a nationwide tour working with PWAs (people with Aids), promoting my work and the book. To make our two-year tour as comfortable as possible and support us in our more or less ascetic lifestyle, we had purchased a 'home on wheels'. It was an extraordinary home, with an incredible interior —

a full master bedroom with en suite bathroom, a kitchen, a dining room and a lounge.

The big coach always drew a tremendous amount of attention, for not only her size, but her whole package, was impressive. It couldn't help but be a bit ostentatious, and I always found it hard to avoid internal tours of my private space by well-meaning curiosity seekers. The man Darryl had spoken to, Hal McGinnis, was a man to whom it was not easy to say no. A wealthy industrialist from St Louis, Hal was a tall, good-looking Irishman in his late forties. I couldn't help but like his forthright manner from the minute I met him. So, of course, the inevitable happened.

Within a few minutes, I found myself sitting in the lounge of the coach. Hal looked rapt, as he blurted out: 'Whew, I've never been in anything like this in my life. Boy, I wish my wife, Dottie, was here. This is more her style!' I wasn't exactly sure what that meant, but it didn't take long to find out. On the spot, he said, 'I want this coach!' He then proceeded to tell Darryl and I that he had the pride of his life tied up to a dock at the St Petersburg Yacht Club.

His blue-water catamaran, *Heart Light*, was named after the Neil Diamond song 'Turn On Your Heart Light'. Made of solid GRP fibreglass, she was built in England to Lloyds of London and Hal McGinnis specifications. Her hull number was 18. With her one-piece hull and snap-on top deck, she had been built to take on the worst the fierce northern seas had to offer. So confident was the designer, Tom Lack, in his design that he offered $10,000 cash to anyone who could *fly* a hull in one of his cats. To my knowledge, flying a hull had never been done until we did it three times during 'the storm'. Tom, if you're reading this, you owe us $30,000.

Personally overseeing the construction on frequent visits to England, Hal had every conceivable option, gadget and toy put on this pure floating decadence. When completed, *Heart Light* arrived like a treasure of King Tutankhamen, sitting high atop a cargo ship, towering above the Atlantic on her virgin voyage.

Tragedy struck for Hal when, on the very first cruise, one of the two women he loved refused to have anything to do with the other. After a beautiful trip to their destination, a not-so-beautiful storm rolled in while they were at anchorage. When that nightmarish storm had passed the next morning, Hal's wife refused to set foot on 'that yacht' again. Sadly, Hal placed his second love, *Heart Light*, at the St Petersburg Yacht Club, and hired a captain to keep her in pristine condition and run her engines from time to time.

The following day, Darryl and I stepped aboard *Heart Light*. We had agreed to look at Hal's highly regarded treasure, if for nothing more than curiosity. Without speaking to each other, we walked around the boat in deep contemplation for the rest of the afternoon. Meeting occasionally in the lounge area, still pensively quiet, I would smile at Darryl. He didn't smile back. Finally, some time after dark, I fell asleep on a bunk in one of the state rooms.

During 20 years of marriage, Darryl had selflessly given up his personal dreams and schemes to follow and protect his woman who was obsessed with finding the holy grail contained within human consciousness. It was the character of his great inner strength that had drawn me to him. We were married within three weeks of meeting each other even though we were both deeply involved in other relationships.

At an early age, Darryl was the creator and proprietor

of 15 successful clothing stores called General Pants, throughout the western part of the United States. He had the gift of making 'a silk purse out of a sow's ear' in business. Darryl found his talent as a marketing consultant served him well as we constantly moved from one location on the planet to another due to my quest. He became known as a 'hip shooter' in marketing circles.

Early next morning, I opened my eyes to see Darryl standing next to me. Looking down, his first words were: 'Are you completely out of your mind?'

Darryl and I had never sailed a boat before. We didn't know the first thing about it. The fact that I had received a very clear vision in an earlier meditation that we would not be finishing the book tour didn't help matters. When I had told Darryl that we would be leaving the country, he had, of course, assumed we would be flying through the air, not skimming through liquid air. Rubbing my eyes awake, I smiled and sheepishly replied, 'Think of it as a new adventure'.

To stabilize himself over the years of living with my kaleidoscopic existence, Darryl had begun working with the I (pronounced ee) Ching, one of the most accepted and recognized oracles in the world. Developed in China over 5000 years ago, the I Ching contains the whole of the human experience, and is used for divination and as a pathway for exploring the unconscious. When properly interpreted, it guides in finding solutions to difficult problems and life situations. Scholars, psychologists, poets, and scientists, alike, have revered its moral and psychological depth, and it was as close to an acceptable source of explanation of the unknown as Darryl could accept at that time. The I Ching had become his only true source of assurance, outside of himself, to help him comply with what seemed sometimes to be the outlandish.

Poor Darryl. On consulting the I Ching about trading his secure land yacht for the dubious sea yacht, he was told to 'cross the great water' and to have 'faith in the unseen'. He would 'not be without demonstration'. He would 'experience great joy and success with his new adventure'.

We called Hal and within an hour were unloading our large motor home with huge storage compartments into one motel room. It was a nightmare! By the time it was done, we couldn't find the bed. At the end of the day I sat on a box and wailed: 'What have I done?' Then, as now, I am amazed at how new ideas always seem so easy in my imagination, but the physical doing can bring me to a different, abrupt reality.

We knew that the secret to our new adventure was to 'push off' the dock! So in April 1989, after refitting the entire yacht and choosing a new name — *Pleiades Child*, after the star constellation — we turned south out of Florida to the open sea. (In May 1994, three weeks before we sailed into 'the storm', I received instructions from within to change the yacht's name back to *Heart Light*.)

I soon realized that I didn't like the unending physical emphasis involved with being on a yacht. Darryl's lack of experience and insecurity as to 'what the hell he was doing out there', meant he was constantly after me. 'Grab this.' 'Do that.' 'Move faster.' 'Where are you going?'

After a jittery trip off Cuba, we proceeded to the Cayman Islands, where we stayed ten wonderful days trying to build up courage to go on. Finally, we 'pounded' our way to the Panama Canal in 12-foot confused seas.

On the fifth day, lack of sleep and food brought on some quite funny hallucinations. I experienced jumping up and down out of my body, trying to avoid the constant slamming of the waves as they jarred the boat. That was when Darryl started his constant reiteration of 'Are we having *fun* yet?' He was especially keen on that question when we had a bell-ringer — when the yacht slammed off the top of such a disagreeable wave that the ship's bell rang one loud 'ding' that shivered all the way up the mast.

We arrived in Panama just before the Bush administration's 1989 invasion to oust President Noriega. Ready for some land adventure after 10 days of uncooperative seas, we were told not to leave the yacht compound. However, my guidance told me that this was to be our first learning curve in the consciousness and conditions existing outside the United States of America. Like exploring children, we crouched on cab floors as we escaped. Once beyond the compound, we were inundated by questions from confused people. What they were being told by their media about events was contrasting sharply with what the American public was being told. Returning to the compound each evening, we saw people like pawns in a hopeless game between uncaring factions.

With enlightened, but sad hearts, we set sail again in early June, heading for the Galapagos Islands after a thoroughly exhilarating experience going through the Panama Canal locks and lakes.

Darryl conveniently got seasick any time he had to go inside the yacht, especially anywhere near the galley. To him it seemed the only thing I did well was cook, clean and my watch. At that time, all I had to do on my watch was sit there and stare at the compass, and make sure we didn't hit anything!

One evening, just off the first of the Galapagos Islands, I was sitting on the swivel captain's chair at the outside steering station totally engrossed in the beauty of the island and water glistening in moon beams. There was just the lightest of breezes. At about 3 am, I was watching the huge golden ball of the moon off the *port bow* of the boat. Slowly it moved to be on the *starboard bow*. Then it was over off the *starboard side*, then off the *starboard stern* of the boat.

Apprehensively, I awoke Darryl to tell him. At first, he didn't believe me. But, when I said I was quite sure that either the boat had gone in a half circle or the moon had gone crazy, he finally came up to take a look. To this day, he doesn't believe that I didn't touch anything!

When Darryl had consulted the I Ching in Florida, we had been promised 'extraordinary demonstrations'. As our grand yacht increasingly diminished in the waves of a grander horizon, all the demonstrations from what could only be considered a Higher Power were formidable. And they had started even before we left Florida.

Darryl and I were unexpectedly taken to a psychic fair and presented with a string of tickets. A bit of a sceptic, I slowly moved through the crowd. Some booths had large gatherings of people around them; other booth-holders sat keeping their self-images in check as they were passed by. I had all these tickets, but had never heard of any of the *readers*. However, the thing I dislike more than a *pseudo psychic* is standing in a line, so I pulled up an empty chair in front of a booth with no clients. In good humour, I said: 'Hi. Tell me something I don't know.' And she did!

She immediately started hugging herself, rubbing her arms with her hands as she stared at me and said: 'Oh, you've been up — up there — you've been up. They are going to contact you soon, then you will be able to put your childhood experiences to rest and know. You've been up, do you understand?'

I nodded my head yes, but I lied. Why can't they ever

speak plain English? Why do they seem to talk in riddles? I couldn't help myself as I coyly asked, 'Do you know where *they* are going to contact me?'

When she replied it was as though she had hit me in the solar plexus. 'At sea; they will contact you at sea. Do you understand?' This woman had no way of knowing I was leaving Florida on a yacht, let alone about my childhood experience of being *up there*!

'Do you know — can you give me the coordinates?' I stammered. She started rubbing her arms again and said she wasn't getting a clear message as she tried to prattle off some longitudes and latitudes. She was looking at me. I saw fear come into her eyes as she said, 'I've never had an experience like this before. Who are you?' I thanked her, stood up and compassionately looked at her as I started to leave. 'That's what I am trying to remember,' were my parting words.

At the age of four, I was taken aboard a spacecraft, today referred to as an unidentified flying object (UFO). Later understandings of this event did not create within me feelings of being special, just different. It took me nearly 30 years to come to grips with that experience, then over 15 more years to understand what had happened. It was completely incomprehensible for my young mind to understand at the time. In later years, it was too taboo to discuss with anyone, until I married Darryl. The topic seems to be more in vogue and even mainstream in today's world of ever-changing controversy.

In the material world I see myself as a pragmatist. If you say you can walk on water, I will give you the total benefit of the doubt. Though, you will, of course, have to show me! I am also a mentalist and an *empath* with the gift of a *seer*. Even so, I felt quite shaken as I related my experience to Darryl. Of course, all he wanted to know was the exact coordinates, but I could remember only some of the longitude numbers. Not too surprisingly, these turned out to be very close to correct.

Months later, some 600 miles off the coast of South America, Darryl and I were making up our nightly bed in the cockpit about 10:00 pm. Since my 180-degree moon affair, rain or stars, the cockpit was now the only place Darryl felt safe sleeping when I was on watch. I felt a bit put out. However, I never got lonely. Mind you, he never got any sleep. We were facing each other, folding a tarpaulin, when Darryl's face suddenly went white. As his knees weakened, I grabbed him and tried to support him. I thought he was having a heart attack, his father having died from one at a younger age than Darryl now was.

Darryl struggled against me. Absolutely speechless and making funny little screeching noises, he grabbed me by the nape of the neck and twisted me around to face the direction he was facing. My mouth dropped open. My heart began to race. The black night was completely covered in a thick layer of cloud, and there, moving like a speeding bullet, directly off the starboard bow was a huge, stupendous, colossal, enormous, gigantic fluorescent green *spaceship*. The actual distance was distorted by the size and speed of the object. It didn't make a whisper as it circled us, dwarfing the yacht.

There are no words to describe the size or the speed of this massive ship. It was only a few hundred feet above the water-line. When it had completed its full circle around the yacht, it shot straight up into the clouds, lighting them up with explosions of colour that reminded me of a fireworks display. The great ship burst through the clouds and disappeared.

At that time, Darryl had been the only one I had ever told about my experiences during and since childhood. He had always graced me with love, understanding, and acceptance. He believed in life on other planets and space travel and, since childhood, had had many unexplainable dreams. However, there was always a little whispering doubt in his mind about what I said. This one event was worth more than all the empty words in the universe. He now faced the same problem I had faced all my life — do we tell anyone? 'No' was our response.

From that night on, at 10:00 pm sharp, what looked like a strobe light appeared in the sky in exactly the same location off the starboard stern of the boat. Even when we changed course, it was still in the same position. At first, we thought it was perhaps a satellite. However, it would flash its brilliant white light through cloud-covered nights. For the first week or so it was eerie, but after a while the light became an expected part of our expedition.

When we arrived in Bora Bora, we heard that the crew of an English yacht, *Can Can*, had seen what looked like a huge green spaceship off in the distance on their starboard side. They were only a few miles south of us at the time.

After this experience, we were headed southwest on what migrant yachties commonly call the 'milk run', the main cruising doorway to the South Pacific from the Panama Canal. We had been at sea for just three weeks and hadn't had time to learn how to navigate. Totally dependent on our satellite navigational equipment, we never realized how big the Pacific Ocean truly was until we sailed for ten long days without seeing land. It was during this leg of the journey that I decided to print T-shirts that read 'CRUISING IS EITHER BORING OR TOTALLY TERRIFYING'.

It was mid-June and we were finally experiencing the previously elusive South Pacific trade winds. We relished steady 20-knot winds with following 15-foot seas. Even though the motion of the yacht was kind and gentle, it was constant. Day and night our unaccustomed bodies moved with the motion of the boat, not allowing us to focus our minds for long on anything else. The skies were a constant beautiful blue. The seas were a constant beautiful blue. Within days, we lost our distinction between sea and sky. After a few weeks, it became monotonous.

One day, Darryl yelled, 'Whales'. It was an extraordinary sight. There must have been more than 100 large pilot whales surfing through the waves coming straight for the yacht. As they drew nearer, I sensed a very dark energy and told Darryl to be alert. I didn't feel these wonderful creatures were joining us in the same spirit that earlier pods of dolphins had.

The whales surrounded the boat, never venturing too close and never cruising the bow wave, but I still had this inexplicable feeling that we were in imminent danger. Then some of the larger males started becoming bolder, brushing along the sides of the hulls. Clinging to the side of *Pleiades Child (Heart Light)*, I made my way to the bow, where I sat down and dangled my legs over the front. I then began to call to the whales, chanting a sound of divine tones and frequencies.

Finally, one of them swam directly under my feet, rolled over on its massive side and looked me straight in the eyes. I kept calling and chanting. Then one by one, for about an hour, they came, rolling over under my feet to look at me. I finally started to feel a bit easier. However, at no time was there the playful energy of our previous dolphin encounters. Then, as suddenly as they came, they submerged to the deep and were gone.

Later in Tahiti, we learned that another American couple had had their boat rammed and holed by a pod of pilot whales. The couple barely managed to get into their life-raft before the yacht sank 1500 miles from the nearest landfall. After checking our log, we discovered that they had been sunk only hours after we had had our encounter, some 14 miles away!

We have since learned that pilot whale pods are very territorial, having hunting areas of several hundred square miles. These incidents are only two of many that have occurred in recent years in the same area of ocean. With larger brains than most mammals and great intelligence, we feel that the pilot whales have been sending powerful messages to the human race, mirroring their own plight from the senseless killings of their family members in drift nets.

Eleven days later we spotted a speck on the horizon. It was the ancient, tiny domain of Fatahiva, part of the French Marquesas Islands. You cannot imagine the thrill of being at sea for three weeks with nothing but sky and water, and then all of a sudden, right where it's supposed to be, is this little dot of land in all that vast blue. We did it! We actually found land out there. In awe, we realized that in a blink of an eye or a slip of a pencil we could have missed it.

Several weeks later, we arrived at a little atoll called Ahé in the Tuamotus chain. We finally found the diminutive entrance through the atoll's surrounding reef, but couldn't understand what we were seeing. The water was virtually boiling. There was no wind and we were running under our engines. Pensively, Darryl said: 'It's getting dark out. I think we should try going in and see what happens.'

Much to my chagrin, he very slowly nosed the boat into the narrow passage. We could feel it start to jitter under our feet, and I felt a cold creepy feeling start to climb my spine. Then, from nowhere, came an unexplainable single burst of wind. It hit the side of the boat with such tremendous force that we spun around 180 degrees, and found ourselves instantly being dragged backwards through the seething waterway at seven knots. We were sucked through, straight as an arrow, before the boat unexpectedly turned 60 degrees to face the anchorage less than a mile away. As we motored gently towards the anchorage, we could see half a dozen waving yachties cheering us.

Darryl and I looked at each other in disbelief. 'Well, this ought to be interesting. Will you tell them you're a genius or the truth — it was by the hand of God?' I asked. Months later, we heard about this genius who knew how to take a cat through a 'riptide' by spinning the boat in the middle and motoring backwards! It is a small community out there.

Finally, in mid-October, we reached the Kingdom of Tonga. We knew we had to leave in the first part of November to make a safe passage to New Zealand through the 'seasonal window' that allows yachts to pass optimistically between the tropical hurricane season of the South Pacific Islands and the northern gales off the top of New Zealand. Both can be deadly.

We were still by no means seasoned sailors and realized that, if we were to encounter any such meteorological event, we would be totally unprepared. To make things worse, we had come to completely rely on 'George', our Cetrek autopilot. Even after 11,000 miles under our hulls, we had rarely taken over the helm, except while motoring through anchorages or docking.

When we had encountered our first major storm between American Samoa and Tonga, we were at a complete loss. Darryl, in a state of panic, sat at the indoor steering station peering into the dark at the faintly illuminated instruments.

The wind was howling 40 to 45 knots. We were in 20-foot head seas and taking heavy amounts of green water over the top. Water was smashing into the upper windows and shooting down the decks into the cockpit. Worse, we were surrounded by reefs — Tonga on one side, Fiji on the other. We didn't have the sea room to run with the storm and get relief.

I kept waiting for the infamous, 'Are we having *fun* yet?', but disappointingly received only silence. Finally, Darryl said, 'I don't know what to do or how to steer the boat if the autopilot gives out'.

'George seems to have everything under control,' I replied. 'Why don't you lay down on the settee.' I turned on the cassette player and played a meditative tape.

Unable to resist the urge to go outside, I found myself standing in the dark, hanging on to the main sheet amongst the crashing waves. Feeling anger at the universe for putting my beloved in such a state, I doubled my fists and shook them at the mounting seas while the outdoor speakers blared the sound of the 'Om' through the howling wind. Unexpectedly, I felt a surge of power pour through my breast as if on some deep level of my stratum I was setting myself free from the elements. I felt that I was in charge and not them. Soaking wet, I returned to the cabin and told Darryl he need not fear: 'The powers that be are taking care of us'. He breathed a half-hearted sigh.

It was early November. We had to muster the courage to cross the greatest and most notorious seas we had yet to encounter. Darryl and I were quite anxious. All his yachty buddies, realising our vulnerability, were very supportive and even protective of us. They told us what to do, when to go, and what course to follow. They would beckon us to leave with them as they left one by one, confident that they had picked the right timing. Meanwhile, we sat waiting for Sage clearance.

Since leaving Florida, I had asked for Sage clearance in every port of departure. I would sit and mediate at 5:00 am each morning. Darryl would awaken later and ask, 'Today?' I would shake my head, 'Not yet'.

As we waited in Tonga, my negative reply was being met with increasingly disapproving and confused stares. He would have to rise yet again and meekly tell his cruising buddies that we weren't ready to leave, without offering an understandable explanation. As time went on, all our seasoned cruising friends left and we found ourselves alone in the anchorage except for another catamaran captained by a retired commercial pilot. Each day, Darryl and he would watch the satellite printout from the pilot's weather fax and then discuss the best time to leave.

One evening, Darryl apprehensively said: 'The weather just isn't cooperating with us now. We should have left with the pack. Are you sure you know what you're doing this time? It's getting late in the season.' All I could do was look at him and say, 'I hope so'.

At 6 am the following morning, I excitedly woke Darryl: 'Get up sleepy head. We're off to New Zealand.' Half asleep, he smiled, then almost leapt from the bunk. But his delight turned to dismay just as quickly when he looked out the window. The wind was blowing torrents of rain on to the boat as she danced around her mooring. Fear replaced excitement. As he had done many months earlier, he asked, 'Are you out of your mind?'

Wrapped in his rain gear, Darryl scrambled into the slippery dinghy and motored over to his pilot friend on the

Prout Snow Goose-designed catamaran. From the weather fax, they decided that there was no way we should be leaving at this time. The Prout was definitely not leaving and Darryl came back determined that we weren't either.

But, even though Darryl put his firmest chin forward, I was in one of those *no room for argument* spaces. We were leaving! I was more terrified of ever going against the Sage than I was of any earthly logic.

We pulled anchor and pummelled our way out to sea in a six-foot swell. Outside the anchorage, the seas increased to 15 feet. However, within three hours of leaving port, the sun came out and we flew through *a window in time* with 25 to 30 knots of wind and beam seas all the way to New Zealand.

As we sailed into Auckland, full of vigour and ready for our next adventure, the crews of the yachts that had left several days before us were still recuperating from their trip. They had encountered 30-foot seas and 35- to 40-knot headwinds. One week later, the Snow Goose arrived to report it had had one of its worst crossings since leaving the United States.

Later, Darryl confided: 'I will never doubt the Sage again!'

Chapter 4

Just call me 'Storm'

Sunday 29 May 1994
■ Approximately 8:30 am ■

'**W**hy are you pushing me so hard to leave? I haven't even checked with the Sage. I am exhausted. We just spent $40,000 in the last seven weeks redoing the entire interior and refrigeration of this boat for Creative Contact. I have been living in mounds of sawdust, boards and nails in every nook and cranny.'

As I spoke, I became aware of the high emotional octaves in my voice. 'We have been back in the water less than 24 hours,' I continued. 'Not only haven't I got everything put away, I haven't even had time to buy groceries! What is going on with you? You have never been this obsessive about leaving port before. You are driving me nuts!'

'Creative Contact' was a venture Darryl and I had been building with *Heart Light* over the last few years. People keen to experience higher consciousness would book *Heart Light* for a week or ten days, and we would take them to a remote area, where there was no electrical or people pollution, for self-development in undisturbed tranquillity. I had become adept at moving energy fields known as kundalini. Helped by high-tech frequency equipment and four years at university studying self-awareness techniques, we were getting amazing results. This was the first year we were fully booked.

Somewhat perplexed, Darryl responded to my plight: 'I just have this feeling we have to get under way. I've been talking to Keri Keri Radio and Jon says that the weather conditions are near perfect. There is a high-pressure system stuck over the south of New Zealand, creating steady trade winds blowing in the right direction for a change. This is too good an opportunity to pass up. The Tongan fleet is leaving, and I want to be with them when they arrive in Tonga. Remember, there's safety in numbers. If you'll start checking with the Sage, I'll help you get organized. That way we can leave tomorrow. This may be one of the first crossings we can actually relax and enjoy, especially with Shane and Shali on board. They've never sailed before and, with these weather conditions, they aren't as likely to get seasick.'

Thanks to our Creative Contact venture, Darryl and I were now commuting between New Zealand and the islands every six months. Even though the Sage continuously provided us with safe timing, it was nonetheless almost always an uncomfortable crossing.

I touched the wisp of hair falling on Darryl's brow, getting in touch with how much I loved this man. 'All right, I'll ask the Sage tonight. I guess if the weather is this good we could put things away while under way,' I acquiesced. I knew he was also tired and anxious to get some free time in Tonga before the first bookings arrived.

Later that evening, after everything had quietened down, I did as I promised and went into concentration to enquire about leaving. I received ominous feelings and pictures. I immediately reported to Darryl. 'I'm sorry, we just can't leave tomorrow; the conditions are not right.'

Darryl looked at me with astonishment. 'What do you mean *the conditions* are not right? *The conditions* have *never* been better. Maybe, it's something going on in you? Honestly, Diviana, the weather conditions have never been this good on any passage we've ever taken from or to New Zealand in the last five years!'

'I'm sorry. That's what I have received. I'll ask again tomorrow,' I responded flatly, feeling quite bewildered by it all. I didn't know what else to say.

I awoke next morning to the VHF radio blurting out praises of weather conditions for all craft. That was followed by the single side-band radio as Darryl spoke to Jon at Keri Keri: 'Yes, Darryl, the weather couldn't be better. However, make sure you take plenty of fuel on board just in case you run out of wind when you reach the thirties, mate.'

Keri Keri Radio is a non-profit private operation run out of the Bay of Islands, New Zealand, by a husband and wife team named Jon and Maureen Cullen. Over the years they have become an institution to all sea-going vessels in the South Pacific. They give ongoing, updated weather reports to all specific areas requested. They also provide a roll call for all cruising yachts who wish to sign up while leaving from or arriving in New Zealand.

I knew what was coming next as I opened my eyes to a beautiful sun-filled morning. 'Diviana, can you hear the radio reports?'

'Yes dear, I'll ask now. Turn the noise down.' I sat up, closed my eyes and prayed for divine guidance. A little while later, I emerged from my cabin and sheepishly stated, 'We can't leave today'.

Darryl shrugged his shoulders and gave me my morning hug. 'Oh well, I'll help you get organized today.

We can leave tomorrow. But, we are leaving tomorrow!'

At this point, I knew that there was more going on in him than I had earlier realized; something that even he was not aware of. Perfect weather or no perfect weather, I sensed a rigidity in Darryl that I had not experienced before. Over the years I had watched him struggle with his logic when I or the I Ching would ask him to trust in what seemed to him and his supporters to be an illogical act or decision. However, his resistance had always been replaced with gratitude when the situation worked out to his favour.

I could fill books with amazing stories of demonstrations and predictions from the Sage. I will share one in particular that happened just a couple of years earlier. We were waiting for Sage clearance while anchored at Kawau Island off the coast of New Zealand. We had been sitting for days and Darryl was getting very embarrassed as, each day, he did his roll call check-in to Keri Keri from Kawau, instead of with the rest of the fleet, which had left a full week before. Jon would say, 'I think you folks should get on your way, Darryl.' And Darryl would have to make up some lame excuse as to why we were still sitting around.

One morning he came in and said, 'At least ask if we can leave here and go on up to the Bay of Islands to wait'. I received a positive and off we went. The following day, his patience at an end, and even more embarrassed as he listened to the nightly roll call from the successfully crossing yachts, he decided we were leaving. However, he promised to check with the I Ching first. His reading turned out to be the fourth line in the oracle: '*Waiting*. The situation is extremely dangerous. It is of utmost gravity now — a matter of life and death. Bloodshed seems imminent. There is no going forward or backward.'

I watched his face turn pallid as he read. For quite a while he pondered what he had read and then suddenly jumped up from where he was sitting and declared, 'That's it. I am going to shake this whole boat down again from top to bottom. If it's not the weather, then it has to be something on the boat.'

Less than an hour later, he returned to the main salon and, with a little embarrassment, exclaimed: 'I found it. The I Ching was right. We could have been doomed if we had left. When I changed out the packing glands, I don't know how I did it, but I didn't tighten down the nuts properly. They were barely on. I must have set them on the bolts so as not to lose them and then forgot.'

I stared at him and quipped, 'In English please'.

'In other words, the nuts would have fallen off from the turning of the shaft, the stuffing boxes would have come apart, and gallons of sea water would have poured in!'

'Oooh oooh,' was all I could respond, grateful that he had sorted the problem out. Sure enough, that evening I was given the coveted Sage clearance, and off we headed for Fiji bright and early.

During the last few years of cruising throughout the South Pacific, we had been blessed to meet wonderful new and supportive friends. We found the sea to be 'the great equalizer'. For the most part, petty prejudices of nationality, dogma, social status, and wealth are replaced by a common need to serve and survive. Not only the elements, but failing engines, refrigeration and everything else that can and does happen thousands of miles from the nearest service outlet brought people together.

I was not as socially inspired as Darryl, preferring meditative states of quiet with self and nature. When Darryl would bring back his new-found allies to the boat, my usual pattern was to make up snacks and serve drinks before slowly retreating to the sanctuary of my cabin, leaving the cheerful party in the cockpit to tell their endless sea stories well into the night.

After countless people asked: 'What was your name again?' or 'How do you spell that?' I would jovially respond, 'My name is Diviana but you can call me Storm!'

I had studied the highly respected works of Professor Jose Arguelles, *The Mayan Factor* and *Dreamspell*. He has dedicated his life to interpreting the mysteries of the Mayan culture. He spent endless hours decoding the Mayan calendar and published a tool called the Dreamspell Wheel. Through a precise process one can track, through one's birth date, an understanding of where one fits into the Mayan mapping of consciousness. However, only one position can be attained, as in astrology. There are 20 named positions on the wheel. My position is called *Cauac, Electric Blue Storm*, the Omega. Interestingly, Darryl is called *Ahau, Yellow Crystal Sun*, the Alpha. These frequencies represent the end and the beginning, through which all transitory human consciousness must sooner or later pass in order to ascend.

When, earlier in May 1994, I had received inner guidance to change the yacht's name from *Pleiades Child* back to *Heart Light*, I was also instructed to place the logos of 'Electric Blue Storm' on the yacht. Following my instructions, a local sign company printed colourful decals of a lightning bolt going through a heart. These were placed on the stern of the yacht and on both sides of the 'doghouse'. Little did I realize at the time that I was being given a prophetic symbol for *Heart Light*.

With Darryl determined we were leaving the next morning, we spent most of the Monday (30 May) filling shopping carts and lugging bags of supplies down the dock. Shane was busy getting the propane tanks filled. Shali was off trying to get her banking and last-minute details taken care of.

Evening came quickly upon us. I felt that there just weren't enough hours in the day. However, I was glad it was over. To make things easier on us all, Darryl and the crew had gone to pick up pizza for dinner.

I was glad to have the time alone and sit in the quiet for a spell. I lit the new rainbow-coloured candles, each in its own special place around the cabin for maximum effect when lit. I poured myself a glass of wine and sat down, realizing that this was the first time since moving back on to the yacht a few days earlier, that I had had the time to appreciate how beautiful everything was.

Everything glowed as I surveyed what we had created. After the hours spent in varnishing, all the fine mahogany now glistened in the candlelight. My favourite addition was the new fabric — varying shades of teal with large sun faces embroidered in gold lamé thread. The handsome faces now sparkled in the dim light.

Being a catamaran, *Heart Light* had a large lounge area with ample shelves and flat surfaces, which I delighted in filling with my natural crystal collection. A few were rare; all were irreplaceable. I spent hours moving them from one shelf to another to find just the right place. Now they radiated out their light and frequencies, creating prisms on the walls and ceiling. The room literally glowed.

There was one crystal that was particularly special to me. Weighing over 65 pounds, its multi-terminated points were naturally shaped in the likeness of my beloved San Juan mountains back home in Colorado. I had worked for many years with the powerful energies stored and emitted by this dear friend, and it now sat in its own place of honour. Darryl and I used to giggle as other cruisers, not realizing they were talking about us, told stories about a cruising cat with people on board who used a huge crystal to get them where they were going because they didn't know how to navigate.

Pictures that were emotionally significant to me were spread throughout the cabin. Two large Joseph Pavsek originals hung over the lounge and had their own special lighting for just such occasions as this night. We found them in Hawaii back in 1976 before the artist found world fame, paying a few thousand dollars for each. I could not imagine what they would be worth today.

Both had been uniquely created on eight layers of glass, each layer painted slightly differently to give the painting tremendous depth. During the day, as the sun's fickle moods changed, so did the depth of these exquisite paintings. At night, they would glow in a third-dimensional fantasy under their spotlights.

A friend had brought us some little stars, suns, and moon stickers that glowed in the dark. Now they, too, added their own special flavour to the whole ambience. *Heart Light* was such a stable platform, all I ever needed was a little double-sided tape to keep things in place during the crossings, even in 20-foot swells.

The scene was exquisite. If you hadn't come through the cockpit door, you would have never known you were on a yacht. As I listened to the warm tones of music filling the air, I breathed it all in and at last felt at peace with what I had gone through to get to this moment. All the years of work to pay for it all: the hours of claustrophobic inconvenience, the endless cleaning of sawdust, now worth this one moment in time. For it would be the only one I would ever be given. One memory to last me a lifetime.

Chapter 5

Destiny or Fate?

Tuesday 31 May 1994

Full of positive expectations, Darryl waited for me to communicate. 'Well, what did the Sage say?'

Feeling his intensity I meagrely responded, 'I got the same black picture. But before you go off half-cocked, why don't you ask the I Ching. Remember the stuffing boxes?!'

Looking away from me he replied, 'Yes, but you're saying it's the weather'.

'Well, that's what I'm getting,' I retorted. 'I don't have a crystal ball. Besides, I am starting to pick up something else that runs a lot deeper than weather patterns. Something's going on. I don't understand why I am only able to skirt it, but something . . . ,' my voice trailed off.

Now at full attention he asked softly, 'What do you mean?'

'I am not sure yet, but whenever I get near it I start to feel joy, then terror, excitement then sadness. It's been very strange. Maybe the I Ching can give us some clarity. I think you should ask about leaving and I should ask for some third-dimensional clarity on whatever it is that I'm not fully getting yet.'

We sat down together on the bed in our new rear stateroom. Darryl asked me to go first. I received:

The Clinging Fire (first line).
'The traces of one's impressions run crisscross. Activity and haste prevail. It is important then to preserve inner composure and not to allow oneself to be swept along by the bustle of life. If one is serious and composed, one can acquire the clarity of mind needed for coming to terms with the innumerable impressions that pour in. It is precisely at the beginning that serious concentration is important, because the beginning holds the seed of all that is to follow.'

And

Dispersion (top line).
'The idea of the dissolving of a man's blood means the dispersion of that which might lead to bloodshed and wounds, i.e., avoidance of danger. But here the thought is not that a man avoids difficulties for himself alone, but rather that he rescues his kin — helps them to get away before danger comes, or to keep at a distance from an existing danger, or to find a way out of a danger that is already upon them. In this way he does what is right.'

Feeling a bit blown away by these readings, I went to *A New Interpretation For Modern Times*, a book by Sam Reifler, and looked up 'Dispersion'. It stated: 'The spontaneity and impulsiveness that accompany your enlightened perspective will carry you to the edge of personal physical danger. A Buddha nature would move calmly ahead and be destroyed. If you retain or recall an iota of the illusion of self, you can easily, safely escape the danger. Saving yourself is not backsliding into egotism. Continue on your egoless way.'

I felt a cold chill run up my spine as I said to Darryl, 'I don't think we should plan on leaving. Now you ask.' Darryl received:

Obstruction (second line).
'Ordinarily it is best to go around an obstacle and try to overcome it along the line of least resistance. But there is one instance in which a man must go out to meet the trouble, even though difficulty piles upon difficulty: this is when the path of duty leads directly to it — in other words, when he cannot act of his own volition but is duty bound to go and seek out danger in the service of a higher cause.'

Totally baffled, Darryl asked for more clarity and received:

Biting through (third line).
'There are great obstacles to be overcome, powerful opponents are to be punished. Though this is arduous, the effort succeeds. But it is necessary to be hard as metal and straight as an arrow to surmount the difficulties.'

'What has this got to do with the weather?' Darryl asked, now more confused and concerned than enlightened by his readings.

Looking deeply into his eyes I responded, 'Nothing, dear. You are being told something totally disassociated with your conceptual questioning. I don't think we should be so impatient to get under way; however, it feels like it's going to be unavoidable.'

At that point, in compromise, we both agreed that, since we had pushed everything to depart that morning, we would leave the berth and head for the serenity of our usual Sage clearance holding anchorage off Kawau Island.

As Darryl was about to go out the door to get his gear

for the showers, he spotted the emergency locator beacon (EPIRB) sitting under the captain's chair. Unscrewing the battery compartment, he said, 'Ya know, I haven't checked the batteries in this thing for a long time. Yep, they're dead as a door nail.'

Never having discussed the EPIRB before, I asked, 'What exactly does that thing do?'

'Well, if you ever had a problem at sea, you'd turn this on and it sends out a signal to a satellite, so that someone can find you,' he responded.

'Well, you'd better run up to the store and get some batteries, don't you think?' I exclaimed.

'It's not that simple, dear. First, you have to take it to a place that specializes in servicing one of these units. Plus the battery costs around $300,' he said.

'You're kidding! For a battery? What the hell are they made out of — pure gold?'

'No, I'm not kidding. Besides, it's going to take at least an hour or more to get the thing fixed, and we need to get under way. We could probably replace it after we leave Tonga and go to Fiji. We've never had to use it. What do you think?'

'I don't know. But after what I've been experiencing and the I Ching readings, maybe we should fix it? If it was just you and me, we wouldn't worry, but we've got the kids with us . . .'

'You're right,' said Darryl interrupting me. 'I'll send Shali down town to get the battery fixed while we fuel up. She's such a cute little girl she could probably get it done in an hour.' And she did.

Ignorance may be bliss, according to the old saying, but on the high seas it can be deadly! Looking back, our guardian angels of destiny are most revered and appreciated.

Before leaving for the showers, Darryl and Shane secured the water toy we had purchased a few days earlier. It was called 'Wild Thing', and it was just that. It weighed around 100 pounds and was about 10 feet long. A space age-looking, solid-glass bottom dinghy with rubber pontoon sides, it was designed for high speeds out to the reefs and for meek-hearted ocean swimmers, like me, who wanted to see the beauty below through its glass bottom. Wild Thing was so big the men had to tie it to the stanchions along the back of the stern. For safety, we never cruised with a dinghy on the davits.

A little later, after Darryl and Shane had returned from the showers on the shore Darryl took me totally by surprise. 'I feel that we should at least go out to Great Barrier Island to wait. It would take six hours off the start of our trip and the conditions are perfect.'

I felt a surge of anger move through me. 'You're still pushing!'

'No, no I'm not. I've been talking to people up at the harbour office and they think we're crazy not to be taking advantage of this weather pattern. I'm not negating what the Sage said. I just feel that, whatever it is, we can wait at the Great Barrier just as well as at Kawau. If we fuel up and get under way we should be able to get into Port Fitzroy before dark without any problem.'

I felt emotionally overwhelmed by the whole situation, especially after three days of going round and round. Darryl had never been this obstinate about moving the boat before. I went to the showers and came back to the boat feeling that whatever was impending was becoming more and more inevitable. Shane and his wife, Shali, were keen to get under way. I seemed to be the only one clinging to the dock. So I surrendered and helped to cast off the lines. After all, it was a beautiful day.

I was very appreciative of the easy sailing conditions for our journey to the Great Barrier. The wind was blowing a steady 25 knots and the seas were on our stern quarter. Even though it was only 60 miles from our departure point, it could become very treacherous in the gulf and channel between Great Barrier and the mainland of New Zealand.

This was the first time that Shane and Shali had been on a yacht, so neither had any experience. And with all the renovations being done on the boat, Shane's arrival from the United States, and his wedding to Shali, we didn't have an opportunity to take them out on a shake-down cruise. This trip would have to be their shake down.

Darryl and I felt that they could learn as they went, as we had. Shane, with his usual unattached mannerism about things, felt that, if we could do it, then it must be a piece of cake. Shali was a bit more apprehensive, mainly over being seasick. She bought and placed an acupressure wrist band on each of her wrists, then took a seasick pill that made her a bit sleepy as soon as we cast off.

I felt the cruise would be character-building for both of them, an opportunity to get away from the pressures of a materialistic society and find peace within themselves on a different level than previously experienced. Shali had been utilizing Creative Contact techniques for growth for about three years, and had moved from being a student to a close friend.

While vacationing in California in June of '93, Shali stayed with us for a while. We had gone back to the United States for a short time to set up promotional connections for Creative Contact. That was when Shane and Shali first met. Then in January of the following year, Shane shifted to New Zealand. They were married in February.

I could hear Darryl showing Shane where everything was and teaching him this and that out in the cockpit under the balmy skies. This seemed a perfect opportunity to take a nap and get some rest; I could put things away at anchorage. Shali was already in her forward bunk. After sleeping for hours, I awoke to find we were just off Port Fitzroy on the northwest side of Great Barrier Island. It was just starting to get dark out.

I went up to the main salon, where Darryl was working on his charts to determine the best angle to go through the narrow pass into the anchorage. Shane and Shali were sitting on the settee talking. Sleepily I greeted everyone and sat up at the indoor steering station, my comfort zone over the years. We were about two miles from the entrance.

Darryl turned the radar on. Looking at the instruments, I said, 'The wind's picked up to a steady 28 knots with a few 30-knot gusts.'

'I'm just about to put the main down. I wanted to get maximum speed before we turned to go in and before it gets much darker out,' came the response.

The sails were set 'wing and wing' or 'gull winged', which means that the main sail is out to one side of the yacht and the jib sail is out on the other side to maximize capture of the following winds. I have always thought that seeing a yacht wing and wing is the most beautiful sight, just as the name suggests.

Suddenly, there was a deafening sound. The whole boat lurched with unbelievable force. 'My God,' I screamed, lunging into the cockpit at the same time as Darryl. 'Shane, get out here, now!' Darryl yelled.

We had gybed when the wind had changed direction without warning. Even with the gybe preventer securely tied, a 45-knot gust had slammed into the mainsail, back-winding it with tremendous force across the back of the boat. And instead of dying back down, the wind stayed at a constant 40 knots with rising gusts. We were out of control.

I ran back inside, jumped on to the captain's seat, started the engines, took the autopilot off and turned the boat into the wind. The comfortable following seas were now foreboding. The yacht was bucking up and down, crashing into nine-foot head seas, slamming mercilessly to the bottom of the short chop, only to rise and fall again.

Frantically, I fought to get the boat in 'irons' as rain started pouring down. The rain had made our plight worse, but what made it critical was having to stay in irons. I was driving the yacht into the wind, bearing down on to the jagged rocky coastline of Great Barrier, now less than a mile and a half in front of us!

Freakishly, and what seemed instantaneously, it became pitch black outside. As I watched the radar screen, the land mass loomed threateningly closer and closer. I could hear Darryl desperately shouting, trying to direct Shane above the thunderous noise of the thrashing sail and the howling wind and rain. Poor Shane didn't have a clue as to what he was being told to do. Suddenly, I heard him shriek in pain, and with great force the yacht lurched once again.

Darryl had handed Shane one of the sheets to cleat but Shane didn't understand. He thought he was to hold the rope. The force of the wind was greater than his strength, and the rope burned the skin off his hands as it pulled away from him, back-winding the sail again and almost taking my son with it. I shouted at Shali, who was still sitting on the settee, 'Get outside and help them.' I couldn't leave the wheel.

The yacht was crashing, the wind was howling, and the

noise was unbelievable. We were in peril. I couldn't believe it! In over 16,000 miles of blue-water sailing we had never gybed. What I didn't know at the time was that the force of the wind had been so great that the new wind-generator poles had snapped like twigs. Not only were the men trying to get the main under control, but also tie off the wind generator before it was driven through the hull!

Darryl poked his head through the door to bark some orders at me. I yelled back, 'Now we're having *fun*!' He didn't reply.

Finally, we managed to get the boat under control. Still shaking, Darryl came in and set a course out to sea away from Great Barrier Island. The rain had not ceased, the wind had not calmed, and the seas were building in the channel. There was no way for us to enter the anchorage. We were being forced out to sea and a greater fate.

Chapter 6

All is Well – All is at Peace

Wednesday 1 June 1994
■ Approximately 10:00 am ■

Still feeling unsettled from the events off Great Barrier Island the night before, Darryl and I sat discussing what had happened. Neither of us had slept during the night, choosing to take the all-night deck watch so that Shane and Shali could sleep.

Before she went to bed, I had asked Shali if she was all right. She said she really didn't know there was any danger until I yelled at her to get outside and help. She had no idea of the magnitude, so it wasn't any big deal in her mind. In this case, ignorance was bliss.

I had also asked Shane how he was doing and, true to his character, he said, smiling, 'Cool. I learned how to cleat a rope tonight and why'. In his 29 years on the planet, this was the first time we had ever been in jeopardy together. Unfortunately, we never know how we or anyone will react under real duress, until it happens. Shane just seemed to take it all in his stride.

At daylight, Darryl assessed the damage. He found

pop-rivets lying at the base of the mast. The gust of wind had been so fierce that the sail track had separated from the mast. Luckily, we had a rivet gun aboard and Darryl was able to carry out makeshift repairs he felt would hold until we got into port. He also tied the wind generator down and felt it would also hold till Tonga, especially since the weather conditions had turned for the better.

We were now a little over 100 miles from the Great Barrier. It was a beautiful sun-lit morning with a steady 22 knots of wind and a following seven- to eight-foot swell. Perfect sailing conditions for *Heart Light* as long as we kept heading north towards Tonga.

We discussed the idea of turning and pounding our way back to New Zealand to make permanent repairs. However, Darryl was convinced that going back would be harder on us and the yacht than continuing with the weather and the fleet to Tonga. We discussed the idea that perhaps what had happened last night was 'the peril' the I Ching had warned us of. However, I didn't feel completely comfortable about that assumption because what we had just been through didn't have the same sort of distinctions the I Ching had defined, especially, the 'higher cause' bit.

As Darryl and I talked, I started to feel a 'strange' calm, more like a surrender, come over me. I wasn't listening to Darryl's logical voice of sea and weather conditions any longer. I was now listening to deep inner feelings that were almost compelling me to keep heading out to sea. I looked at Darryl, interrupting him: 'You never did have a rear-view mirror in your life, so don't start now. What the hell, it's a great day for a sail.'

Standing up and moving his arm and hand as if pulling down on a truck blow horn, Darryl blurted, 'All right!' Giving me a passing kiss, he was off to his chart table. Victory at last, eh?

We had a magnificent day. Darryl, too excited to sleep, plotted his charts, set his instruments and spent the rest of the day teaching Shane as much as he could. Shali spent most of the day in her bunk. She was feeling a little nauseous and had taken another seasick pill which, again, made her sleepy. Doing what I did best on the boat, I made potato salad and fixed sandwiches.

That night everyone took their turn sitting and staring out into the darkness looking for any sign of life that could terminate the peaceful sleep of the others. During our novice cruising days, we had heard horror stories, from well-meaning yachties, about cargo ships demolishing sailing boats in the night without even knowing they had done so. Only floating debris remained the following day.

Darryl and I had timed the sighting of a cargo ship off our bow one night. It took exactly 21 minutes for what seemed to be a low skimming star on the horizon to become a monster dwarfing our little refuge as it crossed in front of us. We tried to hail the imposing ship on the radio to say hello but, to our surprise, got no response. Perhaps radar/radio operators take coffee breaks during the night? Or perhaps they catnap? In any case, that incident kept us solemn enough to make sure someone was always sitting in the captain's chair throughout the night.

After a beautiful sunset, the evening sky was clear. The wind was staying true to its earlier performance and all was well. I could hear Darryl talking on the single sideband radio during his 8 pm roll call to Keri Keri. Confidently, he gave our coordinates and weather conditions. Jon assured him that he had done the right thing in leaving with the last of the fleet and reiterated that he hoped we had plenty of fuel on board.

We had divided the night watch into four shifts. Shali

was to sit and watch from 9 pm till midnight. Shane would then come on until 3 am, at which time I would relieve him. Darryl would start at 6 am. It was important for him to try to sleep during the night. In case of an emergency, he was the one who would have to be fresh.

Each of us had been assigned an orange whistle to be worn around our necks in case of an emergency. I was proud of Shali when, adorned with her whistle, she climbed into the captain's seat at 9 o'clock sharp. Even though she was still very queasy, she said she felt strong enough to do her shift. She asked if she could have a bowl or pan to keep by her side. This was to become her constant companion.

Other than a few rest periods, neither Darryl nor I had had any sleep since Monday night. Even so, I didn't feel comfortable leaving Shali alone on her first night shift, especially when she was feeling ill. So, from time to time, I checked in with her to see how she was doing. Thankfully, I didn't have to leave my comfortable warm bed to do this.

Before the latest renovations, there had been a closet directly across from the indoor steering station. That closet area had been absorbed into the new rear stateroom, which was now our private quarters, but the door had remained. It opened directly on to our new queen-size bed, and was in a perfect location in case of an emergency. Darryl could easily reach the navigation and steering station in one swift move. At sea, we would leave the door latched open during the night so that we could check in from time to time with whoever was on shift only a few feet from us. The real plus for Darryl and me was that, when one of us was on shift, the other could be close at all times.

Thursday 2 June 1994

I had thought that Darryl had managed to get some sleep during the night. However, as he arose to take his 6 am shift, I found out that he too had felt uncomfortable about Shane's and Shali's first night watch, and had barely catnapped all night.

We had another beautiful day, with steady winds and following seas. Darryl's confidence that he had made the right decision was growing. Shali was now starting to get her sea legs as she sat out in the open air of the cockpit enjoying the afternoon sun. I was still concerned that she was not eating and talked her into some fruit yoghurt. Shane, on the other hand, was a bottomless pit. He said it must be the fresh salt air. I felt it was boredom.

That evening, Darryl listened to the radio as some 80 yachts checked in for their nightly roll calls. There seemed to be some concern up around the 24 to 25 latitude mark, close to Minerva Reef. We were hearing mixed weather reports that didn't make any sense, and Keri Keri could find no support for these reports in the forecast records. Jon did not seem too concerned, but he cautioned people to keep him abreast of any new changes. When Darryl checked in, Jon assured him that the forecasts for Friday were still looking very positive.

The lack of sleep over the last few days was starting to show on Darryl. He needed to get some sleep. 'Go to bed!' I insisted, assuring him that we could handle everything just fine. I, too, was feeling tired. However, I had rested more than Darryl during the day, which I felt always gave me an edge on the nights.

I knew we were both feeling a little apprehensive over the mixed weather reports coming from where we were headed, but we didn't speak of it. What was there to say? We were here, rain or shine, and we were now fully committed.

That night, Shali started to feel queazy again. I told her to go to bed; I would take her shift. She had hardly eaten anything and I was constantly pestering her to drink more fluids so she wouldn't dehydrate. However, she wasn't too keen to put anything in her stomach except seasick tablets, which made her sleepy. The sea conditions had been near perfect, creating a stable platform for sea-living conditions on the yacht. Later, I shared my concern with Darryl: 'Lord, if we ever got into some rough water, how in the world would she be able to cope?'

Earlier, I had had a curious intuition about Shali and her wrist bands. When I asked her about them, she pulled her sleeves up to have a look. We found that the wrist bands had all but cut off her circulation, her arms were starting to swell and turn red. I took the bands off and rubbed the deep indentations left by the pressure points. Poor Shali. The bands obviously weren't having a very positive effect on her condition.

I was on Shali's shift only a short time when Shane came up to the steering station. 'Why don't you go to bed, Mom. I'm not tired and you haven't really had any sleep since we left.' I started to argue with him that a six-hour shift was just not reasonable, but he wasn't about to take no for an answer. Gratefully, I joined Darryl in bed.

Normally, there was only Darryl and myself on these crossings. There had been many nights over the last years when I had taken Darryl's shift, not waking him till morning. I took advantage of these nights to meditate while sitting in the captain's chair. I had taught my inner alarm clock to go off every 20 minutes, to the minute, so that I could open my eyes and look at the instruments and the horizon. I would then slip back into bliss. This worked so well that I saw no need to wake Darryl from his peaceful sleep. Shane, however, had youthful stamina, and he had agreed to get me back up to continue the watch if needed.

I lay down next to Darryl. He reached for my hand, and we lay in silence, listening to the waves caressing the hulls. All was well — all was at peace. Darryl started to snore lightly as he drifted into sleep. He always slept more soundly and deeply when I was beside him.

I closed my eyes and moved into a meditative state. This was the first time since leaving New Zealand that I had been in a position to be able to move into my own space, to reconnect myself with my inner source. I could feel my body easily slipping away and the familiar sensation of my pineal gland being activated by cerebral fluids being sent from the pituitary. Feelings of bliss replaced feelings of body weariness as I moved deeper and deeper into inner/outer space.

The depth of my meditative experience had peaked in my physical body several years ago through an explosion of kundalini. I was now able to move freely through inter-dimensional levels of consciousness, levels that I call 'the Kingdom of Heaven'. I understood what Christ had meant when he said, 'In my father's house there are many mansions'.

Most people do not realise we have seven brains operating. Because we have spent the greater part of our evolution developing our lower brains we have no idea of the hidden kingdoms that reside within each of us. Through desire and volition, everyone has the potential to develop their higher brains in order to experience their true heritage.

Through millenniums of time the human brain has evolved into seven inter-connected compartments. Each one is independent in its function from the others even though they are all inter-connected and can and do interact together. The brain is like a musical instrument that has seven octaves. Each octave signifies a higher domain. When you learn to master the *instrument*, you become the *player*.

While experiencing the higher domains several years ago, I started to experience a phenomenon called 'Mudras': that is, involuntary symbolic gestures expressed through the body, face and hands. Darryl had become accustomed to these meditative movements and, at times, would enter into communication with me while I was in these higher states of mind.

He soon learned that it wasn't the same frequency as that of a psychic giving a reading with a crystal ball in hand, which, I think, in the beginning disappointed him. He really wanted to win the lottery just once! Instead, he would receive communication on the nature of the primordial source of all life and new paradigms. He later came to appreciate this knowledge more than all the lotteries in the world.

I had become a 'sensitive' and soon learned that being at sea, miles from any land and its attendant electrical and people pollution, gave me an advantage and greater potential. I had a clear open channel to all the *kingdoms*, with no frequency interference. The night of Thursday 2 June 1994 would prove to be the start of the most incredible journey of my life. The omega and alpha of my own consciousness would manifest before this dream state would end four days later!

CHAPTER 7

A Break in Third-dimensional Reality

FRIDAY 3 JUNE 1994

I awoke to the sound of clamour on the single side-band radio. As I tried to stand up, I realized my consciousness had not fully returned to my body. I felt as though I was looking and listening through a long tunnel to a distant world, which I began to comprehend was the one my body was in. Long ago, I had learned to accept the expanded light waves I experience through my vision that create a glowing ever-changing light field around all matter. However, this morning there was more light than matter.

I was still working on grounding my meditative experiences as I moved towards Darryl. I heard this strange far-away voice coming from somewhere inside my mind asking him, 'Are you okay?' I tried to tune into him as I looked into the field of light energy around him. It was streaked with black/bluish tones, which are not the normal beautiful frequencies I experience in his aura. These tones represented deep-rooted fear.

'It seems there's some reports of possible serious weather ahead of us. But the reports are really confusing. No one seems to know what's happening. It's hard to interpret just what's going on. I've been trying to raise Keri Keri to check with Jon. They must not be on station yet,' Darryl responded.

I knew what was going on in his heart and his mental pictures of what might be coming towards us. I could feel his confusion and fear over his unrelenting driving decision to bring us over 500 miles from the nearest 'bus stop' if there was a problem, especially one he had been warned against. It was the slow dawning of reality creeping up his back as he listened to the radio reports from the Tongan fleet ahead of us; the fleet that he had so desired to catch.

I went outside to the cockpit to feel the freshening wind. I didn't want to further frighten Darryl with my newly acquired knowledge of the event about to take place. I now understood what the Sage and the I Ching had tried to prepare us for. Knowing the passage Darryl was about to experience in his soul, it would have to be dealt with blow by blow if it were to be successful. I could not allow his mind to form irrational concepts and lose the battle before it had begun!

Returning to the cabin, I heard Jon from Keri Keri saying: 'I don't know what's happening for sure, Darryl, but there seems to be some activity up around the 26s. We still don't show a problem here on the weather reports, but we are getting conflicting reports from the Tongan headquarters about deteriorating weather conditions at different coordinates. It's a little strange, but I don't think you have to be too worried at this point. Still being in the low 30s, it might pass you by. I really don't know what to tell you at this time, mate. As soon as I know anything I'll broadcast it.'

'Thanks, Jon. I really appreciate you being there for us. We'll stay in touch if anything changes on our end. This is *Heart Light* clear and standing by.'

Darryl hung up the receiver and went to his charts. After 16,000 miles of off-shore cruising, I knew that Darryl had developed a sixth sense about the weather when at sea. It was this prescience that sprang Darryl into action, checking charts, readying the drogue, pulling the para-anchor out, and the countless other safeguards he would do throughout the rest of the day.

The winds had increased to a steady 30 knots, but the seas were still following at a comfortable 12 feet. Due to the ongoing altered state of consciousness that I was experiencing, I returned to the sanctuary of our cabin. That night, with Shane once again taking Shali's watch, Darryl joined me. He lay beside me, wanting to talk about decisions he was trying to make based on assumptions that he had no information to support. He had only his activated sixth sense with which to work.

'If I start the engines and keep full sails up, we might be able to outrun this sucker. But, on the other hand, if we slow the boat down to a minimum, it might pass us by. What do you think?'

'I think you should do whatever you *feeeeel* you should do,' came my unattached reply.

'God, Diviana. I don't know what I'd do if I blew this one. I mean, it's not such a big deal for you and me, but we've got the kids with us. I mean it might not be anything, but what if the Barrier wasn't the deal? I mean . . .'

'Stop doing this to yourself,' I cut him off. 'Move to

your centre, feel the power of your inner presence. The love that resides in you isn't going to let you down now. Move to trust and ask what you should do. It has always been all well in theory, but now it's *your time to do it*. Try to get some rest now. You might need it,' I added with as much reassuring conviction as I could.

Darryl was too restless to sleep, which concerned me, because I knew he hadn't had more than about seven or eight hours total sleep since we left New Zealand three nights ago. Sometime around midnight he sent Shane to bed. He had decided to 'run'. He had the engines running at a full 2700 rpms with full sails capturing the 30-plus-knot winds. We were a big catamaran and we were now virtually flying through liquid air, with the waves pushing us even faster. I could hear the awesome wake behind the boat creating a rooster tail.

Instead of sitting up at the steering station, Darryl chose to sit on the bed next to me and go out and check on things every 20 minutes. The skies were starting to grow overcast with a thick cloud covering.

I was lying on my stomach and Darryl was talking, however it seemed as if his voice was going further and further away. I found myself moving into a deeper and deeper state of consciousness. Almost in a state of levitation, I turned over on to my back, my hands and arms in full mudra motions. I could feel the psychic electrical energy of kundalini coursing through my spine. My pineal gland felt like a corkscrew going through the top of my head.

It was as if I had become an observer within my own mind. I experienced a pure flow of consciousness freely flowing through my mind and body, but somehow I found another part of myself observing it all. It was like having two minds, both belonging to me, but both working on different levels — one higher and one lower; one tied to my body and brain, one totally disassociated and yet directing the play.

I became aware that one of my floating hands had moved to Darryl sitting on the bed next to me. I could feel psychic energy moving through my right hand into his throat chakra. (A chakra is a major psychic centre, or vortice, to facilitate the consciousness of the residing being. One of our body's seven chakras is in the throat. Planet Earth also has these vortices, as does the entire micro–macro universe.)

Darryl started to cough, but didn't resist in any way as he kept clearing his throat. The throat chakra is directly connected to the fifth brain, where the mind creates and crystallizes concepts. My hand then floated up to another major psychic centre on his forehead. Again, I felt the outpouring of energy. Darryl had become very quiet; no words were spoken. This strange phenomenon went on and off throughout the night.

Saturday 4 June 1994
■ Daybreak ■

The weather had deteriorated seriously during the night. The seas had more than doubled, from a mere 12 feet to a massive 26 feet. I was grateful that they were following us as Darryl and I stepped outside into the rapidly degenerating conditions. Even though I could sense what was coming, I could not have fathomed in my wildest imagination that the seas were just beginning to rise. Astonished by the sky-scraping seas, Darryl immediately went back inside and turned the radio on for any information about the weather, but there were no broadcasts.

To our surprise, we noticed that we had caught and slightly passed two of the fleet yachts during the night. One was now about a mile off our port, the other about a mile off our starboard stern. I tried throughout the day to raise them on the VHF radio, with no response. Being so close, though, they had to know they had company.

Coming back into the cabin, Darryl looked absolutely ashen as he asked Shane to get his wet and safety gear on. He knew something very serious was happening all around him, and I knew he was feeling that his senses were abandoning him on some important level, creating confusion and fear as to what to do.

When he asked me what I thought about the options he presented, I felt great compassion for him as I responded, 'It is your time. You will have to make a choice. What voice will you listen to?' He realized from his experience with me throughout the night that he was not going to get any logical or earthly advice to help relieve his burden.

Moving to our cabin, in a feeling of desperation, he spontaneously reached for the I Ching. He moved to the only other source he could think of to help clarify his present position. He received:

Waiting (top line).
'The waiting is over; the danger can no longer be averted. One falls into the pit and must yield to the inevitable. Everything seems to have been in vain. But precisely in this extremity things can take an unforeseen turn. Without a move on one's own part, there is outside intervention. *At first one cannot be sure of its meaning: is it rescue or is it destruction?* A person in this situation must keep his mind alert and not withdraw into himself with a sulky gesture or refusal, but must greet the new turn with respect. Even

happy turns of fortune often come in a form that at first seems strange to us.'

And:

Preponderance of the Great (sixth line).
'Here is a situation in which the unusual has reached a climax. One is courageous and wishes to accomplish one's task, no matter what happens. This leads into danger. The water rises over one's head. This is the misfortune. But one incurs no blame in giving up one's life that the good and the right may prevail. There are things that are more important than life.'

Without saying a word, Darryl handed me the book as he left the cabin. The deep furrowed look on his face said it all.

■ 8:40 am ■

Darryl went back to the single side-band and started to search for weather information when he heard something that would freeze his heart and take away his last threads of hope that what we were experiencing was just another passing weather front. Across the airwaves came the alarming broadcast of a 'Pan Pan' signal just set off by the yacht *Destiny* heading for Fiji. A Pan is designed to notify emergency traffic when serious trouble is felt. The National Rescue Coordination Centre (NRCC) in Wellington was being alerted.

The Keri Keri radio reports that followed were beginning to sound ominous, confused and a bit apologetic. This storm was coming from out of nowhere! I felt compassion for Jon and Maureen, being placed in the position they were in by giving out the meteorological service weather reports. I wondered how many people would find no other outlet to blame than these two selfless servants at the outcome of this tragedy.

During the height of this storm they were to receive 240 calls from the fleet in a 24-hour period. On top of that, their personal telephone lines were jammed with calls from relatives and friends desperate for news.

Jon and Maureen Cullen had made Keri Keri Radio renowned throughout the South Pacific, becoming the main lifeline to every cruising, fishing and pleasure boat within their vast air space. This is something they do for love of their hobby and the joy it gives them. They have never earned income for the service that so many have become dependent on. The Cullens have now received the Queens Service Medal for community service. And a trust has been formed to raise support money to help relieve Keri Keri radio's financial burden.

However, in our present predicament, it became apparent that the security of the lifeline voice on the other end of the radio was just that, false security! It had also become apparently clear that, in these conditions, there was no safety in numbers. It was time to make life-saving decisions. Suddenly, father and son became equal — man to man, brother to brother. What would they do while trying to find the 'right way', as the increasing swells threatened to pitch them off the boat?

With the wind whining in their ears, Darryl and Shane fought their way to the bow of the boat. They talked about putting a parachute anchor off the bow. Darryl had read a story about a 39-foot Horstman trimaran that survived an 80-foot wave off Cape Horn while anchored to a para-anchor.

Our para-anchor was an 18-foot diameter parachute

that could be tethered to the bow of the yacht by a 150-foot bridle to which 700 feet of line was attached. To deploy the para-anchor and let out the line it is necessary to turn the boat into the head seas, or lie beam on to the seas and drift downwind. And it had to be done before conditions became so bad that those doing the deploying were not placed in serious danger. Once a para-anchor is deployed, you are stuck with it under all circumstances until conditions subside enough to safely pull back the line, unless you were to cut it loose. However, if conditions were that serious, it would be doubtful that you could even get to it let alone cut it.

Heart Light was a luxury catamaran with over-sized windows all around, but especially across the front. She had large windows over the forward bunks and even larger panoramic windows over the lounge area and main cabin. We carried large ply covers for the windows. However, as Darryl tried to nail the covers to the boat, the nails simply bent in half, unable to penetrate the fibreglass. He always said she was built like a steel tank! A little past experience would have been worth its weight in gold. This was an appalling time for Darryl to have to learn these lessons.

At the heart of the storm the windows would prove to be *Heart Light*'s most vulnerable point. The threat of having them punched in by stacking seas would become menacing.

The other option facing Darryl and Shane was to put a drogue anchor off the stern to try and slow the boat down while running with the storm. A drogue is a much smaller version of a parachute anchor. Shane, in his innocence, voted to, 'Go for it. Let's see if we can outrun it.' Father and son agreed and the drogue was deployed. I knew this was our only option. The seas were going to take us to a rendezvous with our destiny.

The hours were passing quickly and the ferocity of the storm was increasing. We were now forced to stay inside the yacht with the cockpit door shut. Shane went forward to rest. Shali was in her bunk. George, the autopilot, was still hanging in there. Feeling a little déjà vu from the last, and only, storm he had ever experienced, Darryl elected to lie down in our cabin with the radio on in case of new information.

■ 11:45 am ■

The radio blared out the coordinates for *Destiny*, further west of us and closer to the centre of the storm. An EPIRB had been set, which could only mean that the yacht and crew were in life-threatening danger.

We later found out *Destiny* had been driven through the top of a massive stacking of waves to find nothing but air beneath her keel. The bow dropped, leaving the crew strapped in the open cockpit feeling weightless. They free fell and dove into the base of the bottom wave.

After so many hours of raging storm noise, they were suddenly under the water where everything was quiet and calm. The crew held their breath until the yacht resurfaced, the agitation of the water tearing at their harnesses and bodies as they were pulled back up into the howling storm.

They had pitch-poled and then rolled. The large antenna tower on the back of the boat and the bow pulpit, both stainless steel, had been bent back directly aft by the force of entering the water. When they rolled, the mast had bent down the starboard side underneath the yacht and come up on the port side. Although *Destiny* miraculously re-emerged right-side up, she had been seriously damaged. The skipper, who had been strapped to the helm, was even more seriously injured.

■ 12:20 pm ■

A Pan Pan was set by the yacht *Mary T* and was being relayed by *Quartermaster*. The *Mary T* was taking on water.

■ 12:23 pm ■

Quartermaster was battling seas and running at four to six knots under bare poles and dragging a drogue.

(The previous evening, while listening to the coordinates of the fleet checking in with Ponsonby Sports Radio in Auckland, I had learned that the two yachts we ran with during the night were *Silver Shadow* and *Quartermaster*. I had cut in after their check-in call and asked *Quartermaster* to turn on their VHF radio.)

'*Quartermaster. Quartermaster.* This is *Heart Light*. Come back,' I spoke expectantly into the mike.

'This is *Quartermaster*,' came the reply.

'Hi Bob. How are you folks doing over there?' I asked.

A very tired and worried Kiwi, Bob Rimmer, responded, 'We're okay at the moment, but it doesn't look too good. We're under bare poles and are trying to slow the boat down with a drogue. How are you doing?'

In jest I replied, 'Well, misery loves company. If you need anything just give us a call.'

There didn't seem to be a whole lot to say. We all knew we were in for it and there wasn't anything we could do or say that was going to make it better.

I told him, being a cat, we would be forced to keep

running and that 'we would catch them on the other side of the rainbow'.

■ 2:05 pm ■

The Royal New Zealand Air Force (RNZAF) were finally able to reach *Destiny*. She had broken her mast in three places and was dragging it through the water, running the risk of punching a hole in the hull. The skipper had broken his ribs and shattered the femur bone in his leg. The only other person aboard, his wife, was in shock and panic, but physically okay. *Destiny* had lost her life-raft, washed away in 70 knot plus winds.

■ 3:48 pm ■

Quartermaster reported they had just placed a bait net out along with the drogue to try and slow down the boat.

■ 3:50 pm ■

Heart Light was still under control and George was still controlling the helm. Darryl had yearned for a cat that could do at least 200 miles a day, but *Heart Light* was a heavy cruising yacht that averaged only about 130 miles per day. However, now his dream was coming true! We were experiencing and living up to the fabled 'quick cat' reputation given to catamarans, though Darryl never envisaged that it would be done under bare poles while dragging a drogue to slow her down.

Clinging to the roller-coaster waves, *Heart Light* flew towards her fate. Like Shali, Darryl had started to lose his stomach, and the stench of endless vomit was now beginning to permeate the cabin. Shane fussed around the galley; it seemed all the excitement made him hungry. He ate throughout the day and night as if there were to be no tomorrow. Shane and Darryl both found it humorous that just watching Shane eat made Darryl feel sicker.

■ 4:15 pm ■

We were startled by a terrible banging sound coming from the cockpit. Darryl looked out the rear cabin window to see that Wild Thing had come unleashed and was living up to its name. He and Shane quickly donned their wet gear and safety lines. Standing with his hand on the door Darryl said to Shane, 'We're going to have to get through the door quick in case we take a wave into the cockpit. It could poop [fill with water] the boat. You ready?' And with that they shot out the door.

I watched them struggle against the wind, now averaging 50 to 55 knots. None of us had been outside in the elements since we shut the door at the onslaught of the storm. I watched them intently to make sure they were all right — as if there was anything I could have done about it.

For the first time, I focused on the storm itself, looking through the window to see stupendously beautiful masses of water towering above our rapidly dwarfing little shelter. The tops of the waves looked like snow-crested mountain peaks as the wind hurled the tops off and turned them into white-capping mountains. The seas had turned to a multitude of colours and depths; greens, blues and white all colliding together. It was glorious. I felt such a resonant vitality, love and oneness for Mother/Goddess and her brilliant ability to capture the attention of all who were obtuse enough to think they had the might to ignore Her reality.

Soaked, Darryl and Shane came quickly back through the door, having done their best to lash the large and heavy dinghy to the floor of the cockpit. One end had been tied to the captain's chair, the other to the stowage lockers. Excited and breathing heavily, Darryl reached for his 'throw-up' bowl.

'There's nothing to hook your safety line on to out there.' Visibly shaken he added, 'We had to cut the wind generator loose.' The wind generator was a very expensive piece of equipment, purchased new a few weeks ago from America and I knew this was very upsetting for Darryl.

For the first time, Shane's cool demeanour wavered as he exclaimed, 'Geeze, you wouldn't believe how big those waves are. I'm not kidding, they're as tall as ten-storey buildings!' And he was right. They had climbed to formidable heights. Who would have ever thought that we would need to have safety lines running inside our cockpit to keep us from being swept off our catamaran? *Heart Light*'s cockpit had become even more treacherous by the fact that it was such a large open area with nothing to hang on to.

With the dinghy now tied as securely as possible, Darryl asked me to go to our cabin with him. He asked Shane to sit at the helm in case something happened to the autopilot. Shali, feeling very seasick, remained in her bunk in the forward cabin.

Darryl and I lay down together on the bed. He spoke softly to me, choosing his words carefully. Trying to be very unafraid, he said: 'I know your birthday isn't for another couple of weeks, but I'm not sure if we, I mean, I feel that maybe I should give you your presents now. How do you feel about that?'

I could tell by the tenderness and love in his voice that he was concerned and afraid that we weren't ever going to see my fiftieth birthday. Lightly, I responded, 'You know me, I never turn down a prezzy. If this is something that you feel is important then I would love to share your gift now, but only on one condition.'

Knowingly, he looked at me, his mood a little more whimsical. 'What do you mean condition? This is a no-condition deal! If you don't want them then that's okay too. You can just wait,' he teased. Before I could answer he said, 'Okay, what's your condition?'

The child in me responded, 'If you give me my presents now, you're not off the hook. You still have to get me a new prezzy in Tonga!'

Knowing I was more serious than not, Darryl laughed, while bellowing his complaint as he scrambled around under the bed to one of his secret hiding places and brought out delicately wrapped packages. He set them down intentionally on his side of the bed so I couldn't get to them. Then he looked at me and said, 'I don't normally give you the most special one first, but I designed this one just for you and only this once, I want you to have it first.'

He handed me the parcel as if it was very fragile. I carefully opened the long narrow beautiful wrappings to find inside a velvet bag with satin drawstrings at the top. I opened it and, to my delight, pulled a two-foot, custom-made crystal wand out of its sheath.

It was a magnificent piece of *functional* artwork. A large chunk of multi-terminated amethyst crystal was set in a large gold handle, about seven inches long, that had been covered in finely woven satin ribbon of gold, violet, and purple. The gold work continued as a hollow brace, set with semi-precious stones of amethyst and natural amitrene, for another six inches or so. It held two magnificent quartz-crystal points, the top one extending out about seven inches beyond the brace work. Both crystals were double terminated on each end and sat about one inch apart.

It was exquisite. This was more than just an art piece. The wand was conducting considerable energy so I knew that the craftsman had known exactly what he was doing. Holding the base, I placed my right hand over the top of the wand to play in its energy field. Now humbled, I looked Darryl deeply in the eyes: 'It's beautiful. Thank you.'

Quite pleased by my obvious response, he told me, 'I had John Alloway make it for me.' Proudly, he continued, 'I told him exactly what I wanted. This wand is to celebrate your transformation.' Then very tenderly he said, 'To me, you are the *Goddess*. I wanted something that would mirror the state of consciousness I experience in you, and what better than an ascension wand?'

I was very moved by the clear intent and effort he had put into this very special gift. He handed me my card:

'Happy Birthday. I love you my darling. Our future is secure because our NOW is perfect. I lay the world at your feet. You can have your heart's grandest desire while you remain embodied. You have broken through human consciousness and now are the expression of God/ Goddess. Let us play and fill our hearts with joy. You are my *Omega*. I AM your *Alpha*. I love you forever. Darryl'

Jostling me to his reality, Darryl handed me another very long and narrow package. Taking the present from him, I looked at him coyly and said, 'Another one. Oh, you really shouldn't have dear, but I'm glad you did'.

This time there was one long, perfectly cut icicle piece of quartz crystal. I had never seen such a long and narrow one-piece cut of stalactite natural crystal. He told me that it was a collector's piece and explained the hard time he had had buying it from its previous owner. However, he had been determined it was to be mine. It was about one and a half feet long and perfect, beautifully perfect. It was splendid to hold and feel its extraordinary energy field.

I set it down and picked up the ascension crystal, saying to Darryl, 'You know quartz crystals are known for storing energy. I have a wonderful idea. Let's absorb as much of the storm as we can into the crystal. You hold the wand with me and we'll focus all our concentration on the storm and store it in the crystals.'

With a flicker of hope in his eyes, as if somehow the crystal could actually absorb enough of the storm to make it go away, Darryl placed his hands with mine around the crystal and concentrated. Soon I could feel the wand start to get hot, so I told him that was enough. I then picked up the stalactite crystal and asked him to do the same thing with me. Saying a prayer, we held the crystal up over our heads, closed our eyes and concentrated. Incredibly, there was a startling high-pitched tone as the crystal exploded at its centre point, sending crystal fragments flying in all directions.

'Whoo,' Darryl exclaimed, opening his eyes.

Sadly, I told him that the frequency in the storm must have been too intense for the stalactite. No longer a collector's piece, I put the two pieces back in their velvet bag. I knew Darryl was surprised and disappointed about the crystal shattering. However, oddly enough, he didn't show any emotion about it as he hugged me and went off to check in with Keri Keri. I knew then that he had resigned himself to a negative outcome to our predicament.

■ 6:23 pm ■

'Keri Keri. This is *Heart Light*. Come back,' Darryl spoke into the mike.

'Roger, *Heart Light*. This is Keri Keri. You're loud and clear. Go ahead.'

Darryl gave our coordinates and the alarming weather conditions we were now experiencing. Jon was very concerned, very caring, and sounded like he was feeling quite helpless under the siege of desperate yachts with which he was being faced. 'I don't know what happened, mate. It looks very very bad. It's starting to show up here on the weather reports. It's nothing we've ever seen before. Very very bad. I don't think you're going to avoid this one and I want you to check in frequently from now on. Don't worry about what time it is, just keep checking in.'

'Jon, my wife Storm wants to have a word with you,' Darryl said, handing me the mike.

'Hi, Jon. You and Maureen handling all this okay?' I asked.

'We're doing the best we can under the circumstances, Storm,' he replied.

'Jon, I need you to do me a favour. If you don't hear from us will you please notify my mother in the United States. She doesn't know we've left port yet. And, Jon, you'll have to tell her, I'm sorry, but her grandson is with us.' Thanking him, I gave Jon all the details. 'This is *Heart Light* clear and standing by.'

It was now early evening and there was really nothing

anyone could do. We could hear the ferocity of the storm building outside. The waves were starting to break over the top of the cabin, crashing down on us. George was still valiantly battling to keep *Heart Light* on course, so I told the men that I wanted them to rest. It was going to be a long night, and I would sit at the helm and watch for a while.

As I sat there, a clear telepathic voice said to me, 'Watch George'. Understanding, I stared at the autopilot. I became aware that there was a position flag and a roving needle in one of the little window displays. I watched intensely and I began to realize that the needle position was always giving reference to where the rudders under the boat were.

The seas were quickly building beyond description and, as I watched the speed log, I was amazed at how fast the yacht was plunging, under bare poles, down the face of these towering slopes, while dragging a sea anchor behind her. I could feel the tug of the anchor and then a letting go and then another swift tug as I watched the digital speed log display gyrate between seven and 14 knots as if it were out of control.

I could hear George's electronics squealing under the formidable force of trying to readjust the stern over the failing rudders, and became entranced with how fast or how slow the autopilot would correct the rudders. I sat there for at least an hour watching George do battle. I began to feel like George and I were one synchronized mind. I knew in my heart that it was only a matter of time before the inevitable would happen and Darryl would start to encounter his own worst nightmare.

One loud continuous squeal and, suddenly, all my equilibrium was lost as *Heart Light* was violently thrown sideways, beam to the mammoth wave she had been battling. The yacht lurched, sliding sideways down the face of the wave, free of her drogue for the moment. As she slid to the bottom of the trough, Darryl sprang from the bed. He grabbed the wheel and fought to correct the direction of the boat as I turned off George.

Righting the boat, he turned George back on. I told him of my experience of George over the last hour. He looked at me with a resigned expression, as if to say, so what has that got to do with reality, and went back to his bed.

Shane had quickly emerged from his forward cabin. 'Woooo, that was scary. What happened?'

I told him as he clung to the captain's bench for stability. I also told him of my experience with George. He thought that was 'very cool'. His attitude amazed me. Here he was, facing his own possible mortality, and all he could say was, 'very cool'?

For an hour, I mimicked what I had experienced the autopilot do after being continuously overwhelmed, and each time I managed to bring the yacht about, except for one. That brought Shane forward again. He offered to take over and to try his hand at keeping George on track.

No sooner had Shane taken over the helm than we got swamped again. Taking my breath away, *Heart Light* lurched sideways and Shane exclaimed, 'Ooooooh shiiiiit!' Like a cat, Darryl arrived, landing on his feet, grabbing the wheel and struggling over Shane to bring the boat right.

Shane climbed out of the seat and Darryl replaced him. No sooner had Darryl reset the autopilot than we were again overwhelmed. It was becoming obvious that this storm was about to demand the personal presence of our 'reluctant' skipper. It was time for Darryl to face reality.

Chapter 8

War in Heaven, Hell on the High Seas

Saturday 4 June 1994
■ Approximately 8:00 pm ■

Still fully experiencing my altered state of consciousness, I was having visions of floating angelic beings surrounding me. One stayed directly within my inner vision at all times as if tattooed to my inner forehead. Sometime during the evening, I had a clear inner voice that had become an echoing repetition: 'The Kingdom of Heaven is near at hand'.

Throughout the day, I had started hearing and listening to a profusion of high-pitched sounds. It was like a radio picking up more than one signal at a time, with many voices trying to talk over the top of each other. At times, there were fleeting periods of clarity. I knew the prophetic war of consciousness for third-dimensional reality had begun and, during it, Darryl would battle for his soul.

My attention turned to Darryl, who was still sitting at the helm. He had had a reprieve, as George took over the helm once again. With anguish in his voice, Darryl blurted out, 'Diviana, if I have to drive this boat, we might as well kiss our ass goodbye!'

Very steadily, I looked at him and said, 'You haven't tried, and I agree with you. If the Darryl Wheeler sitting in that seat has to take over this helm, we might as well kiss it goodbye! You are in a state of total self-obsession, full of fear and self-pity. We don't have time to deal with your self-indulgences.

'*You* have to make a choice, right now! Are you just a man or are you more than that? You think you've spent two-thirds of your life chasing me around this planet. In reality, you have been chasing *you*, that greater part of yourself.

'By the grace of God you are being given the chance to experience who you really are. Remember what the I Ching told you: "There are more important things than losing one's own life'? Well, this may be one of them — it's up to you.'

Suddenly and spontaneously, I grabbed the cushion Darryl was sitting on and, with a tremendous surge of strength, jerked it out from underneath him.

'When you were a kid you thought you were the hottest, baddest driver on ice. All I ever heard about was wheelies and donuts from days of glory being raised in Alaska. This is no different. Think about it. Visualize it. Feeeeeel it! Place your consciousness in your butt sitting on that seat! Connect with this boat. Pretend like you are sitting in your Pontiac GTO. Feel it. It's no different. You're on ice. Love it. Play with it. Be a kid again. Fly by the seat of your pants. If we are going to go, let's have some fun doing it!'

Without warning, slam! We were hit with enormous force as a monstrous wave crashed down into the cockpit with inconceivable force. The front half of the yacht was now airborne as gallons of water crashed into *Heart Light*, shoving her sideways. She was careening sideways down the face of a mountainous wave as Darryl took over the helm.

I yelled at him over the roar of the wave, 'Can you *feel* it? You're on ice.'

He started rotating the wheel back and forth like a racing car driver. We hit bottom and started up the other side. Miraculously, he brought her back on course. I could see pure exhilaration in his eyes.

'Now, that wasn't so bad was it?' I teasingly asked. We both burst out laughing. Shane, who had managed to struggle his way into the main lounge, joined our madness and said, 'Let's rock and roll', which made us all laugh even harder.

I repeated my experience with George, telling Darryl that the secret seemed to be in not over-steering the boat — catching it as soon as the autopilot failed and before the boat could get away from him. Concentrating as I had done earlier, Darryl now started tweaking the little dials of George's manual controls. He focused all his concentration on the compass and the little flags in the rudder viewer while we listened to the single side-band.

■ 8:20 pm ■

The yacht *Sofia* reported losing her self-steering and was under bare poles in very rough seas.

■ 9:12 pm ■

Mary T was experiencing rain, thunder, and lightning. Her cockpit had started to leak. They asked if someone would notify their 76-year-old mother, but only if necessary.

■ 9:20 pm ■

A mayday relay came across for the yacht *Blue Inwar*, on a reef somewhere off Fiji. There were no injuries, and so far no holes. They had put together a survival kit, and were asking for a rescue team to be sent as soon as possible.

■ Approximately 10:00 pm ■

The sound of the storm was now raging outside and the motion of the yacht had become taxing. It was like thrashing around inside a washing machine while going down a roller-coaster track. In surreal bursts of pure energy, lightning would shatter the black void we hurtled through, illuminating a frenzied seascape of mountainous sea and white spray streaming horizontally in the night.

We were now experiencing hurricane-force winds 65 to 70 knots strong. Massive unstable waves were breaking and pouring hundreds of tons of water down on *Heart Light*, which could not escape the avalanche. The yacht would dive, then pitch as if being tossed like a Tonka toy down the now-dreaded seaways. As I sat next to him on the captain's bench, Darryl complained about being tired. He had not slept for over 30 hours. His eyes were starting to affect him as he stared at the dimly lit instruments.

I had him move forward in the seat and wrapped myself around his body, embryo-style, on the wooden bench. I started to talk to him as I rubbed the back of his shoulder and neck: 'You must blend with my energy my love. Pull from my strength. You and I are one; we always have been. Remember, when we first met and we took that long drive across the Arizona desert?'

Darryl was silent so I continued: 'We made up and played that game where we decided we were so much alike that we would have more fun being one androgynous body. Remember, we spent hours arguing over which body parts we would keep between us? Now I want you to feel that oneness. Receive the strength of the Goddess. Know that you are cradled and loved and not alone out here.

'I haven't told you this yet, but we are heading for a vortex. We are going to meet brothers and sisters there from a much higher dimension than this Earth plane. We are going to transcend this world together, mentally or physically, it doesn't matter. Your job is to get us there. You must break through your human ego to do it. There are forces in this storm that are trying to stop us from reaching the centre of the vortex.'

I could feel his tiredness and resistance to what I was saying. He knew better than to think me mad. He had admitted that he, too, was hearing 'the voices'. Earlier, I had heard Shane ask his father if he could hear strange sounds or voices all around them. Darryl had said he could. When Shane asked me, I confirmed that he was hearing inter-dimensional voices, but assured him that he needn't worry. I did not want to frighten him any further, and could not see the point in trying to explain the unexplainable at that time.

I could feel Darryl's love, but he was still distant and

more resigned to his own demise than the thought of being reborn a Divine Being. He was listening to me on one level and, on another, to another part of himself — his own ego, that was not about to release control of him. Very tenderly, I said: 'Listen to me. You know there are no accidents in this world. We are responsible for our own *videos*, no matter how much we try to blame circumstances or luck. You chose to be here during this extraordinary event.

'Think about it. You chose to be here. You knew in your heart you were ready. It was your time to join with me, blend with me, become "The God/Goddess potential". This is your *storm — your battle*. Tune into what is going on around you. You can hear the voices! Why do you think we are here? Do you think that all we are has been abandoned or that we are being punished for some proverbial sin?

'You have been called to come forth and choose between your DNA-encoded body and brain or your Godself. Your lower brain is telling you that you are a pawn in the human drama, about to die and lose your family; a victim in this storm. You are listening not only to your voice, but you have tapped into a "collective lower frequency stream" of voices that are trying to control you through your emotions.

'Wake up, Darryl. You know that your consciousness is part of the whole collective field that surrounds this planet. You know that body you are clinging to so desperately is nothing more than a holographic field. Feel, remember who you are, what you are and where you are. It is your time; you chose it — wake up!'

'Enough,' Darryl interrupted. 'Enough!' He just sat there staring into space. I could feel my energy start to amp up as I fought for his consciousness. I continued:

'There is nothing limiting you except you! Where is your precious logic now? Who is going to save you now?

'You brought us here — fight, damn you, fight. Get mad. Feel hate. Feel the truth. But feel something now!' I screamed at him as I sat up and looked at him.

His eyes were like burning coals. He reached for his bowl, vomiting. I put my arms around him and said, 'Throw the fear up, Darryl. It won't serve you. Throw it up. Get it out of your body.'

He retched loudly, literally spewing the word 'FEEEEEAAAAAARRRR, FEEAARR'. As he retched over and over, I cooed to him: 'That's it, my love. Get it all out; all of it. I love you. You are your own phoenix and you shall rise out of your own ashes.'

Shane, concerned over the shouting, had emerged from his cabin. I asked him to take Daddy's bowl and get him a towel. Darryl was sweating profusely.

'This is not just your battle,' I continued, when without warning, there was a hideous whining noise like someone hitting the wrong key on a heavy-metal guitar with the amplifier full on. I felt my body free-falling through the air as I was thrown across the yacht.

The first impact I felt was hitting the wall; the second was Darryl's full weight slamming into me. Never have I ever seen so much pure adrenalin in action as Darryl scrambled for the wheel to bring *Heart Light* back under control. I wasn't moving so fast, my body racked with pain. I didn't know the extent of my injuries and so chose to take time to find out.

A terrible crash had also come from Shali's stateroom. She had been thrown from her bunk high above the floor and was pitched into the wall before hitting the floor and being buried under everything that came with her.

We had broached. Our port hull had left its roller-coaster track and flown up into the air at least 80 degrees, trashing the contents on the entire port side of the boat as everything that was not tied down became a flying missile. The refrigerator contents were strewn half-way across the yacht. Broken glass was everywhere, which would soon become a real threat. Flour mixed with broken bottles of juice had created an explosion of thick sticky paste that coated everything. Aloe vera juice, tofu, honey, and breakfast cereals coated the walls. And my beloved crystals were buried under a mountain of debris and peanut butter. We later found tapes, which had started the voyage in drawers in the main cabin, in the lower hull sections.

Shali crawled from her cabin to the main lounge floor. 'Be careful of the broken glass,' I warned her. She looked terrible. She was in pain and didn't seem to comprehend what was happening. She was terribly and deeply bruised from her shoulder down to her thigh and legs. There was nothing anyone could do for her. Bravely, she said, 'Don't worry, I'm all right.' She then started vomiting. She hadn't eaten anything, other than one small cup of yoghurt, in four days and had taken little or no fluids, and yet she continued to vomit pure bile mixed with blood.

It had become apparent that Darryl could not stay in the captain's seat on his own. There was no harness to strap him and no holding brackets we could tie him down to. I went to his side and looked deeply into him. His short-lived confidence had completely vanished. He was being attacked from the inside out by his own terror. And to add to his terror, Shane, looking out the window yelled, 'Wild Thing's loose!'

Wild Thing was now flying its own hull in the cockpit. It had torn loose from one of its tethers and was now standing straight up on one pontoon while being held by a single rope tied to the outside captain's chair. It was banging against *Heart Light*'s cabin wall. I could feel Darryl's panic from the potential outcome of this new incident.

Without a word, Shane grabbed his safety harness, as his Dad said, 'Where do you think you're going?'

'Someone has to go out and tie it back down, and you sure as hell can't leave the wheel and do it!'

Darryl started to argue, but Shane just cut him off as he reached for the door saying, 'Look, Dad. The bottom line is I'm expendable; you're not. If you go, we all go anyway. I've got nothing to lose.' With that, he went out the door.

Darryl couldn't take his eyes off the instruments, even for a minute. He yelled at me, 'Watch him through the window. Tell me everything you see . . . Well, what do you see?'

'Hardly anything,' I responded, 'I can scarcely see anything. There is so much spray and darkness.'

Suddenly, there was a horrifying crash and we felt *Heart Light*'s cabin wall shunt forward and then snap back. Darryl, realizing we had just taken a major wave into the cockpit shouted, 'My God, Diviana, is he still there? Can you see him? Is he still there? Shane!' he cried, shackled to *Heart Light*'s wheel.

From out of the cockpit came the sweetest sound we could hope for. We heard Shane bellow at the seas that had tried to snatch him from the cockpit: 'Fuck you . . . fuck you!'

A few minutes later, with the dinghy tied back down, a soaked and bruised Shane came quickly through the door. 'This storm is flat starting to piss me off!' he said angrily.

Darryl, reaching one hand forward to touch his son, asked, 'What happened?'

Shane started to grin and said, 'Man, this awesome wave came flying into the cockpit, slamming me against the cabin wall. And when it tried to take me out to sea with it, somehow I managed to grab the cockpit carpet and hang on to it. I was underwater in the cockpit. The carpet lifted up under me and I managed to grab hold of it. The drain-holes sucked the water, carpet and me back down to the floor.'

Looking at his son incredulously, Darryl could only manage to say, 'Thanks, son. Go get some dry clothes on.'

Darryl got on the radio and called Jon: 'Keri Keri. This is *Heart Light*. Come back.'

'How you doing, Darryl?,' a very worried sounding Jon Cullen came back.

'We just had our first serious broach, Jon. Pretty scary stuff,' Darryl gravely replied.

After we gave our coordinates and abominable weather report, Jon told Darryl that he now wanted us to check in every hour on the hour throughout the night. He and Maureen had set up a bed in the radio room and were taking turns throughout the night to keep up with all the distressed yacht's coordinates in case of an emergency.

Darryl despondently hung up the mike. It was as if he could just somehow keep talking to someone on the other end, everything would be okay. He looked worn and tired as deep depression started to move through his energy field and show on his face.

Shane had worked his way back up to the helm. I called to him. Sitting next to me on the floor I whispered to him, 'I think I'm all right, but I don't want to move right now. You will have to take over and hold your Dad in the captain's seat. Don't say anything to him about me other than I am fine, do you understand?'

'Yes, Mother,' he replied. 'But I want you to know that I feel we are fighting something much more powerful than just this storm. I think something *out there* is trying to kill us and I'm not talking about the storm.'

I looked at him and told him it would be all right: 'The Kingdom of Heaven is very near now. We are heading for a vortex. We are being protected. Have faith. Truly, it'll be all right, no matter what the outcome of this illusion is to be. Now go to your father and hold him in his seat and do not let him fall out again, no matter what!'

He smiled at me with such tenderness and understanding that he actually glowed. I had such love for this boy/man kneeling by my side that it was hard to contain it all. His courage and willingness to do whatever was asked of him filled my heart with respect and appreciation as I watched him talk to his dad. And then like a football linebacker, he pressed his shoulders into his father's body, wrapping his arms around him to hold him in place. They almost looked as if they were dance partners.

'I haven't seen you two boys get this close in years!' I teased mischievously.

Darryl responded by grabbing his bowl and spewing vomit through the words 'TIIIRRREEEDDD'. Again and again, he spewed his tiredness out into the bowl. When he was finished he said that he actually thought that the 'fear trick' worked so he might as well try it on his tiredness.

Shane, half laughing through his seriousness expressed, 'Ooouuh, I can't stand this. Mom, I can't take the bowl to the galley. I can do almost anything, but this is the one thing I can't take!'

I struggled back up to my feet and staggered towards the galley. I didn't make it. To the horrendous shambles of food, glass, furnishings, clothing and other assorted debris was added the contents of the bowl, which went skidding into a corner as I reeled with the impact of yet another wave.

Seeking somewhere stable, I removed some of the debris from the settee to make a spot I could lay down on. To my surprise, it was soaked. Every square inch of the entire settee was waterlogged. Where was all the water coming from?

The water was now about toe deep in the main cabin from the force of the waves being driven through the door from the cockpit. However, there was no way it could have reached the settee. Pushing it from my mind, I lay down on the cold wet fabric, deciding not to add to our worries by saying anything to the men.

■ 11:46 pm ■

Bob Rimmer on *Quartermaster* called in a mayday. They had rolled violently 360 degrees. He also reported that his wife, Marie, had received a one-inch cut above her eye during an earlier knockdown.

■ 11:55 pm ■

A Pan Pan was set by *Arosa*, now under bare poles.

Sunday 5 June 1994

■ 00:10 am ■

Mary T was working under emergency tiller. A crew member had hurt his back.

■ 00:35 am ■

'*Quartermaster* — Keri Keri — Roger, you're loud and clear. Go ahead.'

'We just took another knockdown, Jon. I don't know what to do,' came the reply from a painfully unnerved skipper at his wits' end.

'No, there's not much you can do. How's everybody on board? Is anybody hurt?' Jon came back.

'No, we're just hanging on, Jon, we're just hanging on.'

Their GPS (Global Positioning Satellite) still showed 0 on the screen after being frozen from the first knockdown, making it impossible for them to give Keri Keri their position coordinates.

The storm around *Heart Light* was still building! Winds now averaged 77 knots with gusts shooting up to 90 knots and holding. I called out from the settee: 'Darryl, think about what I have been telling you. I am in frequency (a term Darryl and I used to describe higher states of mind). You have to listen to what I have been telling you. You only have a very short time to surrender to your own higher being — the goddess within you; not me, but in *you*.'

He said something under his breath to Shane, who was still unswervingly holding his father in his seat.

I knew that the opposing forces had finally found our location in the storm. Their dark presence, manifesting in lightning and thunderous sounds, was all around us. We were becoming the centre of the battlefield. I could hear the myriad of voices like a mixed radio station fighting for airwave dominance.

The blackness outside the windows would light up as bright as daylight. Hideous apparitions were moving around the outside of the yacht as if trying to gain entry. Thunderous bedlam was now surrounding us. The power of the wind was forcing one wave on top of another, stacking three high to heights of 100 feet or more before breaking, like a tsunami, over the top of us.

Through this eerie heinous state of activity, Darryl started to transform his comprehension, as if my words were becoming manifest in some way that his earlier human perception could not accept. But now, being in the middle of it, living it, he understood. He started to become aware of the truth of our situation. He was starting to wake up, to remember that this was preordained; this was his destiny. This was not just another hurricane or cyclone. This was a battle to the finish for something much greater than any one single human being. This was the battle that would determine the outcome of the human race.

Darryl's warrior spirit started to take over. He yelled at me, electrifying the air: 'I understand, Diviana. I understand. I know what's happening. I know!'

No sooner had he said these words than the starboard hull was being pulled free from its sea floor. Once again, up, up went the hull. This time there was a crashing/crackling sound all around the boat, not only from the inside, but from the outside as well. The boat heaved and shimmied as the hull raised higher and higher. I could hear Shane shout at his father, 'You're not coming out of that seat,' as both of them were thrown up on to the yacht instruments and controls just to the left of the steering station.

This broach was more violent than the first one. It felt as if a huge hand or force was lifting the hull up and out of the water, higher and higher, almost in slow motion at first, with the hull shimmying and struggling against it.

We could hear the grotesque shattering sound of the fibreglass twisting and flexing to it's breaking point. It was as if these forces were now trying to twist the boat in half!

Suddenly, *Heart Light* was set free from the powerful grip and snapped back with a terrible hideous noise and force that sent the contents of the entire yacht flying in all directions. Shali, sitting on the floor clinging to the side of the settee, disappeared. She slid across the floor, down two steps into the galley and head first into the refrigerator on the port side of the boat.

There wasn't one thing that escaped destruction. The pictures were wrenched off the walls, breaking their glass frames. Rivets were flying with glass and everything else conceivable on a yacht that had been set up like a floating condominium. It looked like a bomb had exploded inside the boat!

Darryl screamed at the force. 'You son of a bitch, STOP IT, STOP IT NOW!' he commanded.

In response to Darryl's outrage, the force of the wind surged and swept past 90 knots on the knot meter. We could feel the pressure against the cabin of the boat and wondered if it would hold together.

'Holy shit,' Shane yelled.

Darryl started to laugh as he shouted, 'Maybe I need to try a different tack: PPPLLEEEAAASSEE stop,' he screamed. The three of us howled with laughter.

Shali reappeared holding her head: 'Did you see my graceful slide across the floor? Now I have a headache and a lump to add to my seasickness, dizziness and the pain from my bruises!' This sent all of us into hysterics.

■ Approximately 1:00 am ■

Darryl contacted Keri Keri and told Maureen we had had our second serious broach. He gave her our coordinates and told her about the immense electrical storm we were in before clearing and standing by. There was no sense in trying to tell anyone about what we were experiencing. They would think we had gone mad under the pressure, and we knew it was just the beginning.

CHAPTER 9

The Kingdom of Heaven is near at Hand

The storm and its supernatural participants were increasing their ferocity.

Destiny was a 45-foot Robert Perry-designed Norseman 447. She was heading for Fiji with experienced cruisers, Dana and Paula Dinius, hailing from Long Beach California, on board. They were hit by this abomination late on Friday night. Shortly after midnight they experienced what they called 'strange shapes appearing in the blown spume. They looked solid enough to touch' as they flashed over and around them.

They said these shapes defied the 70-knot howling winds by freely moving left and right near them as they sat strapped in the open cockpit. They both felt a very 'powerful presence'. Both of them also felt very strongly that they were 'under attack by some entity that was not of nature'! It had swirled around the hatches as if seeking entry into the boat or looking for someone. After satisfying some unknown intent, as suddenly as it appeared, the 'evil presence' moved on, taking with it its unnatural presence 'with its heavy feeling of malignant evil'.

The Dinius' were not alone in their paranormal experiences. The Kiwi yacht *Irresistible* was also on course heading for Fiji when the storm exploded upon them. A very alarmed Paul Everett, one of the crew members, said: 'We were not alone out there'. He and his crew mates were hearing and seeing 'things' coming out of the storm.

One of the crew, who was described as a very large man, was found by the skipper and Paul huddling in the corner of his cabin. He was pale faced and sombre as he said, 'I can hear voices, Captain!' He then put his ear to the bulkhead. 'There they are again.'

Paul also told of how, while on his shift, he experienced 'holographic-like apparitions' floating around in the cockpit. He could quite clearly see faces. He expressed feeling very uncomfortable about telling anyone about it.

New Agers predict a fourth-dimensional shift involving the Earth and her inhabitants. *Something* is going to cause the world to go through a global shift. They believe this will give us the opportunity to create a new world of peace and growth. Those who are willing to raise their personal frequencies through love will be able to make the shift.

Many business leaders also state that the world is going to experience a paradigm shift. This will happen when the world view shifts from its fundamental view of reality to a new lateral perspective.

Others believe that the end of the world is at hand. That a new world will be created for the 'chosen ones' which is just another version of the above. There are over 50 million adult Evangelical Christians in America alone who believe in Armageddon. Every culture in the world teaches some form of change or shift: 'The end time on planet Earth'.

This has been the most dominant and programmed concept in human consciousness for the last 3000 years. There are many versions of this *affirmation*. However, all are explicitly connected together, visibly or invisibly, like tangled skeins of yarn. All are tied intrinsically to the final and decisive battle predicted in the Bible between good and evil. This battle will not be fought like any other previous battle in our conventional world. It will be a battle that takes place between the Forces of Good and Evil in the heavens before filtering down to mankind.

Most people ignore the role religious concepts play in most of the wars taking place on the planet and in world politics. Other wars are created for the financial gain of the super powers behind the scene.

Most people are so completely obsessed with their enslavement to survive the system that they do not take the time to lift their heads out of the quagmire long enough to spread their conscious awareness out into the world in order to get an objective look at what is going on around them. And those that do usually pull back, thinking there is nothing they can do about it anyway. This is the insensibility that has allowed the so-called 'dark forces' to have *carte blanche* in our world. We find it easier to join them than to fight them. Like ignorant children we *buy into* their political madness as we send our children off to fight and die for them. Lest we not forget, we have been taught to make it okay by justifying it in the name of God!

While being deliberately driven out to meet this tempest, I came to the reality that we were now going to experience the skirmish to bring the *Forces of Good* into this world to start the battle for world dominance. This battle had to take place at sea, where the conflicting forces and the ensuing vortex doorway being opened to allow the *Higher Forces* to penetrate through, could take place without tearing the 'prize' asunder.

The I Ching readings were coming into conscious alignment as the dawning of this battle started to unfold: 'There is one instance in which a man must go out to meet the trouble, even though difficulty piles upon difficulty: this is when the path of duty leads directly to it — in other words, when he cannot act of his own volition but is dutybound to go and seek out danger in the service of a higher cause.' 'There are great obstacles to be overcome, powerful opponents are to be punished. Though this is arduous, the effort succeeds. But it is necessary to be hard as metal and straight as an arrow to surmount the difficulties.'

Sunday 5 June 1994

■ 1:10 am ■

It seemed as though *Heart Light* had become an animated living thing. Against all odds, she fought valiantly to hold herself together as if determined to save her family. I watched *Heart Light* and Darryl merge into one entity as if she had become his second skin. Darryl was now in full battle mode as the yet-unbridled storm raged on. We were fighting gyrating 77-knot winds that would suddenly soar and slam into us at 90 knots.

My consciousness was moving deeper and deeper into the etherical levels of the 'clash of forces' trying to break through the third-dimensional fabric. I was receiving profound communications. My brain felt like a computer being downloaded on a disc as I was filled with information, knowledge, and transformation.

Darryl's heart was fully in control of his mind and senses as he released himself into full surrender of the 'Greater Power of himself'. With restored vigour, he drove the boat with the skill of a seasoned world yacht racer as *Heart Light* flew through perilous seas.

Shane held him dauntlessly hour after hour, in awe of his father's ability. As they were being tossed around in the captain's seat, fighting to stay behind the wheel, Darryl kept our yacht on her destined course.

■ 1:12 am ■

A Pan Pan was set by *Tranquillity*. She was taking water on board as she sailed close to Minerva Reef.

Several other yachts were trying to shelter from the storm at Minerva Reef, a reef almost completely covered by water except at low tide. One yacht was dashed against the reef, while others were dragging anchor. Miraculously, they saved themselves by moving around the reef, using it as a buffer from the huge seas throughout the storm.

■ 2:04 am ■

Quartermaster had been knocked down hard again. They had their motors running and were trying desperately to get the seas on their stern quarter.

Maureen took the call: '*Quartermaster*. Keri Keri. Good morning. How are you going out there?'

'We're surviving here but the inside of the boat is a complete shambles. Over.'

'How is everybody coping inside? Over.'

'We're just lying here where we can,' came the reply.

'Roger, Roger. We're just sitting here thinking about you all out there.'

'Thank you very, very much,' replied the exhausted Bob Rimmer.

'Keep your chin up. It's got to improve. This is Keri Keri clear.'

That was the last time Keri Keri or anyone else would ever hear from the courageous *Quartermaster* and her family, who were playing a more vital role in fate than they would realize while in their earthly bodies.

Soon after, I felt a strong presence. I closed my eyes and discovered it was Bob Rimmer. Through my mind I surrounded him, his wife and their son with a veil of golden white light. I had a vision of them. They had been knocked down again, a window had broken out, and the yacht was quickly taking on water. I saw them as they struggled outside to launch their life-raft.

One of the men managed to get inside the raft and set the EPIRB before *Quartermaster* suddenly rolled. Still tied to the yacht, the life-raft was dragged down under the roll of the boat, while the others were instantly set free in the depths of the sea. The air-filled life-raft ripped itself free and jettisoned through the rigging straight up and out of the water. The man in the life-raft was thrown through the top of the rubber safety cover, shredding it and setting him free. It all happened very quickly; there was no pain.

Mercifully, they had not been trapped inside the boat. They were instantly cradled and protected as their spirits were set free to join their own true destiny and return to their pristine home in the *Kingdom of Heaven*. Only then did I realize how prophetic my last words about catching them on the other side of the rainbow had been.

A thunderous wave smashing down on top of *Heart Light* snapped me from my vision as gallons of water gushed through the solar vent, soaking me and my bed. I crawled to a drier corner to wait.

Shane, Shali and Darryl would later write in their journals about this time. Shane wrote: 'As I held my Dad in his seat, I could feel tears well up in my eyes. This was the longest night of my life. Will it ever end? I had thoughts coming to me. It was like many thoughts at one time. I was glad Dad had broken through whatever he was supposed to break through to. At least Mom was quiet; Dad had taken charge. I'm sure that if I had to be in this storm with anybody else driving the boat, it would have capsized.

'I could feel Dad's tiredness as the early hours of the morning wore on and on, hour after hour, with him sitting there staring at the instruments and me holding him. It was like he was on autopilot as time and time again he would struggle to bring *Heart Light* back under control. We were both very tired and there were times when Dad would start to nod off, lean sideways, then catch himself. I didn't know what to do. I felt strange being at his side because I'd never had to give him my strength or this much love, close up like this.

'Mom was in her stateroom. I could hear whispers, many voices, coming from there. Shali was still lying on the cabin floor next to the settee with her teddy bear. She, too, had tried to help Dad by rubbing his back, but she was too weak, too sick to stay long. All I really wanted her to do was empty Dad's and her barf bowls for me. I couldn't stand that and the bowl kept spilling all over. There was barf everywhere!

'My thoughts were taken to the people on the boat. I had a strong thought in my head — which was, I'm expendable. I have to do what is necessary so that the others will survive — especially Dad. He wasn't permitted to get hurt. He was the only one who knew how to sail or drive the boat. If he went down, all would be lost. But if I bit the dust, there would have been hope for the others to survive. I didn't give up on myself; a warrior doesn't give up.'

Shali wrote: 'My admiration for Darryl really increased as he stuck with it, driving the boat through what seemed like hell. The winds were 80 knots with harrowing higher gusts and the sea swells were getting higher and higher. Water was starting to seep through the windows. The two bullet-proof covers placed over the lower front stateroom windows had been ripped from the boat by huge waves crashing down on them. During the Great Barrier experience I had decided that I wouldn't be in fear, hysteria or panic as long as Diviana was calm. If she was to even look worried, then I would panic!

'I felt helpless and weak because I was sick and could only stay upright for a small amount of time before the feeling of nausea caught up and all I wanted to do was to put my head down. Diviana had us create white light around ourselves, the boat, Shane and Darryl. Sometime during the height of the storm on Sunday morning, Darryl made us a promise that he would get us all safely home, and I believed him. He said it with such commitment, conviction and strength that not one of us could doubt that it was to be so. That and Diviana's love gave me the strength to keep going.'

And Darryl wrote: 'Throughout the onslaught of the

storm, Diviana whispered, yelled, and used every means necessary to kick my heart into gear. I watched her beautiful boat and all of her worldly possessions being trashed. Every square inch of the boat and all of her beautiful treasures were smashed and scattered everywhere. Everything we owned in this world, everything we had worked for was in this boat, now disintegrating before my eyes. There was no insurance on the boat or its contents for my mind to fall back on. In the midst of it all she just said, "It doesn't matter. We're birthing a Divine Being here!"

'During the first stages of the storm I felt uncontrollable fear and panic. All I could see was that I was solely responsible. The Sage had warned me. I had stubbornly persisted in leaving and now I was about to die. Worse, I was going to cause the deaths of my most beloved and my family. Guilt consumed me. Fear and tiredness pressed into me from every corner.

'As my self-indulgences engulfed me, a voice kept coming to me. It was Diviana, telling me it was time to transform; time for me to realize who I was; time to emerge from human limitations. I looked at her and thought, "Who in the hell does she think she is?"

'She kept putting her face in mine and relentlessly penetrated deeper and deeper into my eyes, pulling at the very foundation of my soul. The only thought I had at the time was, "Shut the Fuck up!" Reading my mind, she would yell at me, "This is an adventure. You created it by agreeing to be here with it. Live it. Be it. It's glorious. It will set you FREEEEE!" I could feel my mouth opening and words yelling at her, "Enough!"

'She backed off. I sat amongst the chaos surrounding me. I started pondering her words. I knew I was being forced to make a choice. Diviana had demonstrated to me and others for years her uncanny ability to see who people really were. Why couldn't I now accept the fact that she was seeing me as this magnificent being?

'All I could see was fear and panic. I didn't know how to handle the boat. Reading me she shouted over the storm, "I . . . I . . . I . . . me . . . me . . . me . . . That's all I hear coming from your mind. Ask yourself who the *I* and *me* you're listening to is!" Even though I had brought us to the edge of peril, every time I looked into her eyes expecting to see blame or I told you so, all I found was unconditional love. Her commitment was total.

'I decided not to listen to "my" . . . , "these" voices anymore and to try and embrace the thought of who I truly was. As if personally struck by lightning during the electrical storm, something extraordinary happened to my consciousness. It was in a flash of my mind, I understood, almost like a memory or something buried so deep in me that I could catch a glimpse of something so inexplicable that, when it came forward, it was a "major rush". I felt like I had been sleeping and suddenly was being abruptly woken up.

'In that moment, my heart burst forth with a knowingness. I was in control. Nothing and no one, from this world or any other, was going to destroy us. I found this absolute determination and I turned my anger on the storm. I yelled at the storm and the fiendish faces gleaming through the dark windows, "You cannot have my family". I focused and blended my body into the boat. I felt one with her, feeling every move in the massive waves, anticipating and correcting a fraction ahead of the next assault.

'I felt free. I was free, at last. The voices in my head were gone; my fear was gone; no more panic. Confidence from my own higher essence transformed my mind and filled my body and muscles with energy to help stave off the tiredness and pain.

'I became aware that I was not a physical body, but a mental one. No matter what the outcome, I was going to look death in the face and tell it to go to hell! I felt myself melting and merging with Diviana. Armed with a goddess and new-found self-recognition, I found the courage to fight into the night.'

■ 2:30 am ■

The *Tui Cakau*, a cargo ship, had located *Destiny* and was standing by to try to take the crew off at first light. In fighting unfathomable seas to get to the yacht, the *Tui Cakau* had rolled over 40 degrees. Her chief officer suffered a broken leg during another roll as the ship was tossed violently to and fro.

The *Tui Cakau* was not fully loaded so she had about 30 feet from her water-line to the main deck. The bridge deck was another four main-living storeys up from that. The captain reported that standing on his bridge, he was at times aghast while 'looking up' at the crest of waves trying to engulf his ship.

Manoeuvring towards the stricken yacht, the two craft had become totally unpredictable in the confused seas. The captain of the *Tui Cakau* tried to position the huge ship alongside the dwarfed *Destiny* using the classic manoeuvre of trying to keep *Destiny* in his lee so they could attempt a rescue.

A rope was thrown to Paula Dinius for her to cleat off while two very courageous Fijian crewmen were lowered in a life-raft from the *Tui Cakau*. The raft itself was contained in a cargo net. Like a Hollywood stuntman, one of the Fijian rescuers leapt on to *Destiny*'s deck with a stretcher, yelling at the petrified Paula, 'Jump into the raft.' When she hesitated at the sight of *Tui Cakau* rolling precariously, the husky man quickly grabbed Paula and threw her towards the rising life-raft.

Paula just managed to sink her slipping fingertips into the safety net hanging off the side of the raft as the gigantic ship quickly rolled away from the decks of *Destiny*, hurling Paula up with it. The other rescuer, still inside the raft, with life-saving timing, reached over, grabbed her by the seat of the pants and hauled her into the life-raft, now two stories above the decks of *Destiny*.

With the last of his strength, Dana Dinius had managed to drag his broken body into the companionway hatch. He was immediately lashed to a stretcher by his Fijian rescuer. Ropes were dropped down, the stretcher was quickly shackled and then, just as quickly, the stretcher was jerked straight upward towards salvation.

At that moment, *Tui Cakau* was once again rolled by an unwieldy wave, this time towards *Destiny*. Dana was thrust between the hull of the yacht and the hull of the mammoth ship. The stretcher hit the water and then skyrocketed back up as the *Tui Cakau* rolled away. Dana was smashed into the side of the ship, instantly breaking more of his ribs. *Destiny* was being destroyed as the massive ship repeatedly rolled down on her.

■ 3:30 am ■

Sofia activated an EPIRB after being rolled and dismasted. A RNZAF Hercules was dispatched to try to make contact.

Another wave crashed down on *Heart Light*, pouring yet more water through the solar vent on to the bed. There was no dry place left to sit. I crawled out to the main lounge to find a dry place, but there was not a single spot that was not soaked. I then realized my clothes were drenched so it didn't make any real difference.

The violence was increasing. The waves were now missiles of sea, striking their target with deadly accuracy from all sides. I watched in disbelief as one cannonade hit the long window along the starboard side of the boat. As if in slow motion, the window flexed away from its aluminium frame. Shali saw it, too, and I watched her hold her breath as immeasurable gallons of water poured through before the frame snapped back into place.

It was to be an ongoing miracle throughout the dark morning as the frames, held together only by the threads of their pop-rivets, flexed and snapped back after allowing gallons of sea water through. The mystery of where all the water was coming from had been solved, but now didn't seem a good time to say anything to anyone.

From out of the cockpit came a yacht-shattering sound! Shane let go of his father and shone a flashlight out the window. 'Oh my god,' he winced. 'Wild Thing's loose again. I mean really loose'. His voice now filled with fear. 'She's got one rope still tied to the captain's chair and is trying to punch her way into the interior of the boat.'

The cabin shuddered as the dinghy flew forward, slammed against the wheelhouse wall, then retreated and flew forward again with a sickening crunch. Wild Thing had not done this too many times before Shane grabbed a knife and went to the door. I came and stood next to him. As he put his hand on the door handle he just stood there looking at me. His leg was moving very rapidly up and down like he was driving a manual air pump.

'What are you doing?' I asked

'I'm pumping myself up to get the courage to go back out there,' he responded. 'I'm scared, Mom.' I started to say something to him, but he stopped me: 'I'm not afraid to die for you, I'm not. But I want to be able to see your eyes when I go, that's all. I just need to see you!'

I looked him very evenly in his eyes: 'I will hold the light on you. If you start to go, I will come and be with you, I promise you. You won't have to leave alone, do you hear me?'

With that, he shoved with all his might against the weight of the wind pushing against the door and vaulted himself into a terrifying world of blackness, wind, and sea water. I shone the flashlight through the window and saw Shane dodge the flying dinghy. It had become a lethal weapon that could crush anything that got in its way.

He fought the bucking shape still tied to the captain's chair. Unexpectedly, it got away from him and thrashed over the side, threatening to punch a hole in *Heart Light*'s hull: Shane frantically sawed with his knife at the rope holding Wild Thing. Finally, with a mighty snap, the dinghy was freed from its tether and launched into the waiting frothing seas.

Inside, Darryl was yelling, 'What's happening?' his voice filled with concern. Even though the electrical phenomena had ceased, there were still sadistic 50-foot waves all around the boat, each one with the potential to seize this courageous mortal who had dared to venture out into their presence. Again and again Darryl yelled, 'Get him inside,' and still Shane did not appear. 'Get him in here, *now!*' screamed Darryl, his voice raised a pitch.

Shane had crawled back into the cockpit from the top side of the yacht, clinging to the deck for dear life. His focus and determination were to get through the cabin door and the safety within. Just at that moment, though, a large container holding the para-anchor ropes came loose and leapt into the air, hurtling out its contents. Some 600 feet of rope started dancing in the wind like an angry snake thrashing in a frenzy to get away. The rope wrapped around the down-haul on the mainsail boom and entangled itself in the jib sheets. The container with the balance of the rope threatened to hurl itself into the main cabin. Disastrous scenarios emerged.

The rope had become so entangled in the sail boom that the only hope of freeing it quickly was to cut the line. However, Shane knew that by doing so we would have no use of the sails if we survived the storm. Even more frightening was the possibility of the rope going overboard. It would wrap itself around the propellers and we would lose the only stabilizing factor we had left, our engines.

Shane instinctively sensed this and proceeded to try to untangle the disarray. Darryl, still shackled to the wheel, ordered his son back into the safety of the cabin by yelling out the window at the top of his lungs, 'Cut it loose and get back in here, now!'

Shane ignored him and continued to untangle the rope while hanging on to it as mountainous avalanches of water poured down on him. Finally, praying he had left just enough of the boom line to still sail the boat, he cut the rest and threw it overboard. Out of the night, our waterlogged and exhausted son dove back through the door into the refuge of the main cabin.

Darryl wrote about this event: 'When Shane said to his mother that he was not afraid to die for her, but he wanted to be able to see his mother's eyes, I felt my heart burst with love for him. However, the words that followed coming from Diviana's mouth brought every hair on my body to attention. "Do not worry, Shane. I will be there for you if anything happens. I will follow you. You won't be alone, I promise." My mind knew the depth of her commitment and that, if Shane was swept overboard, she *would* follow him. The thought of losing Shane horrified me. The thought that I could lose both of them at the same time, paralyzed my heart in unabated fear.'

Soon after Shane had come back into the cabin, I told Darryl: 'Be prepared. It won't be much longer. We are getting closer to *Heart Light*'s destination. It won't be long now.'

Chapter 10

Tear in the Fabric

Sunday 5 June 1994

■ 3:35 am ■

Following Jon's instructions, we had checked in throughout the long night and morning every hour on the hour to give our coordinates. Darryl could feel the terrible stress Jon and Maureen were under from the events happening throughout that hellish Sunday morning. He could feel their tiredness and feelings of helplessness from listening to friends facing death alone in a black abyss.

I listened to him check in. He tried to lighten their load by giving them appreciation and saying things were under control. He did not tell them the full circumstances we were facing. 'Why didn't you tell them the truth about the wind speed for their records?' I asked.

'What good would it do?' he replied. 'There is nothing they can do and it would just upset them further.'

He was right. What good would it do?

I could hear the tiredness in Darryl's voice. He had not slept in days and had now been on the wheel a straight nine and a half hours, doing what seemed humanly impossible to do.

■ 4:05 am ■

The National Rescue Coordination Centre in New Zealand reported another EPIRB had been set in the area around the yachts *Sofia*, *Takimoana* and *Irresistible*. Two other EPIRBs had also been activated, but the NRCC hadn't been able to get a good fix on their location.

Irresistible had suffered two knockdowns. 'We experienced a tremendous crash that took the yacht over on its side,' said crew member Paul Everett. 'It made an incredible noise along with the sound of smashing crockery and glass. The boat was groaning and screaming, charging through the white foam all around us. The seas would lift *Irresistible* high into the air and then down, what seemed an endless slide. The whiteness and the force of the seas were amazing and we all realized that one false move and we were goners.

'After the knockdowns the sight of vegetables and barley soup was everywhere. We ended up grovelling around on the cabin floor in the dark, slipping and sliding in the soup and broken crockery while *Irresistible* was still reeling and shaking from the force of the knockdown. A huge chunk of silverside left the galley at "mach 6" and flew across the salon, bursting open the shower door and spraying the walls and ceilings as if a mad plasterer had applied stucco.

'The mess was unbelievable; the crew were below shaking from the force of the knockdown. They were huddled together on the port side of the cabin and had become the target for everything that possibly could move from the starboard side. The chart table opened and released its load. The GPS, divider, rulers, charts, pencils, the lot, missiled across the boat.

'We were in an endless journey into the unknown, our lives were in the hands of nature at its wildest, testing all of us at all times.'

■ 4:15 am ■

We were not experiencing any relief. The battle raged outside us. The missiles were direct hits, and the seas were relentless. Even though I was receiving confirmation that we were almost at the centre of the vortex, I questioned how much longer Darryl's body could endure. I had been told that *Heart Light* would 'stop' at the exact centre of the vortex. My lower mind raced trying to imagine what was meant by that. How was a 42-foot cat, flying eight to 13 knots under bare poles down 100-foot stacking waves, going to simply 'stop' in the middle of the Pacific Ocean during one of the worst storms in history?

My only inner response never ceased its mantric tape in my mind: 'What does it matter? Faith and trust; that is all there is. What will be will be. This is what you have come here for. Be with it. *You are it*. The Kingdom of Heaven is near at hand.'

As we drew nearer and nearer to the centre, I felt surrounded by so much love, cradled by 'un-human' hands in such a way that the tears would stream down my face in the humility of what was transpiring all around me. I could now see my brothers and sisters from the Seventh Realm moving in their Etherean ships through the centre of the vortex, using my consciousness as a beacon and a doorway into this dense time loop called third-dimensional reality. I had lived my entire life for this one moment and had not realized that it would come in such glory and be surrounded by such adventure.

We are all inter-dimensional beings. Through our consciousness, whether we are aware of it or not, we embrace the whole of each dimension as one folds over the other. Science explores dimensions through the limitations of time and space. However, a dimension is literally a unique and specific band of frequencies beyond time and space that we can perceive with intelligence. We can experience these dimensions with awareness and mental cognizance.

Taught that the only true reality is what we experience through our physical senses, most of us experience everything in the third dimension through a dense physical body and the human brain, which interprets frequencies through its five senses of sight, sound, taste, smell and touch. Because we utilize our senses to explore density, we have become disillusioned; we believe that everything is separate from ourselves.

Atomic study and quantum physics have proven that everything is inter-connected and inter-related — non-separate. However, most people are still so tied up in the *human drama* of separation, enslavement and dogma, they do not realize the truth about themselves or the reality surrounding them. All outdated deterministic and mechanistic global views have been scientifically disproved and no longer hold any more validity than the Earth being flat. Physicists have proven that materialism is no longer a valid scientific philosophy and that science is now dealing in technology that transcends the physical.

Even though today's scientists are just beginning to learn the truth behind the material world, this knowledge has been available since mankind has been on this planet. It has been and still is being rewritten, distorted and bent to manipulate the masses. This exploitation of the truth through confusion and half-truths has been deliberately done from behind the scenes, to serve the desires of the political few.

■ 4:28 am ■

Darryl checked in with Keri Keri and gave them our latest coordinates. As the savage storm raged on I knew the end was very near. It was time to prepare everyone for their possible physical departure from this world. I called out to them, 'Shane, Shali, come over here please.' They joined me on the floor next to the indoor steering station. Above us, Darryl clung to the wheel, where only the faint glow of the instruments illuminated his face. 'Darryl, can you hear me?' I asked. He looked down, his eyes full of love and a calm surrendered peace, and replied almost in a whisper, 'Yes'.

'We are very close to the centre of the vortex now,' I began. 'It is not yet known whether we are going to take our physical departure there or not. In case we do have to leave, we must prepare ourselves. Now listen carefully to what I am about to tell you. When you were born into this world, you were in your mother's womb, which was filled with salt water. You were safe, cradled, and loved in that environment. Your bodies have that memory stored in them. The minute you release your clinging to them they will immediately go into a state of joy, not fear.

'You have been taught you are not your bodies; you can feel the truth can't you?' I asked as I watched them nod their heads attentively. 'For us to leave our bodies in peace we must focus on this truth. If necessary, together, we will release them in joy.'

I looked at Shane and directed him, 'If the boat starts to go down, it will be your job to open the door, do you understand?'

'Yes, Mother,' he replied.

I knew that if they were caught like rats in a trap with the boat upside down, no way out, and filling with water they might lose their centres and panic. I felt that, if they were kept moving, their minds wouldn't get caught up in fear and they would have a smoother transition.

Tenderly, I continued, 'Then you will all follow me outside back into mother's womb. We will all go swimming, all of us together.'

'And the water's pretty warm where we are now,' quipped Shane.

We all laughed and Shali said, 'Good, I don't like swimming in cold water!'

■ 4:32 am ■

*H*eart *Light* and her unwavering crew were now caught in the wake of this paramount event. We were starting to experience the final death throes as Higher Forces fought to gain entry into this dimensional field and lower forces fought to seal the door.

In one last desperate rage, a force gripped *Heart Light*. Her starboard hull once again started to rise with an ear-shattering cacophony. This was to be the final struggle for control of the gateway by the forces of darkness. We were at the zenith of the battle. As *Heart Light*'s hull raised higher and higher, I called to Darryl: 'We are here. *Heart Light* has found her spot!'

It was as if everything then went into slow motion. Darryl was thrown violently from his captain's seat while the hull lifted higher and higher. With an ear-shattering sound, we heard *Heart Light* roar her final death scream as she careened down a 100-foot wave out of control. It felt like she was being hit from all sides by a freight train.

Still in slow motion — up, up, up she went — 80, 85, 90 degrees. She was now standing straight up with one hull flying through the air. All of us were thrown on to the cabin wall, which had now become the floor. We could feel the forces struggling with the hull as *Heart Light* trembled and quaked under the impact.

Time seemed suspended as we teetered 90 degrees on one hull high above the unstable surface of the sea, free-falling down the slope of the 'liquid Himalayas'. Kneeling on the cabin wall, Darryl looked at me, his eyes full of surrender and peace: 'I did the best I could.'

I looked at Shane. His hand went for the door as he screamed, 'GOD NOOOOO!'

CHAPTER 11

In the Eye of the Vortex

Heart Light's hull was caught in a powerful tractor beam from a Seventh Realm spacecraft hovering above us in the tempest. The dark force that had tried so hard to destroy us was itself now held by that same beam.

I felt my consciousness being expanded outside the limitation of my mind. My body, *Heart Light*, and the entire storm were now being projected inside my inner vision as I watched the drama unfold. My mind became inseparably linked with the occupants of the hovering spacecraft. I was infused with telepathic intelligence.

I watched the crystalline, lens-shaped ship as it hovered less than 300 feet above *Heart Light*. It was surrounded by an etheric green glow that slowly changed to shades of white and orange then back to green. The invisible beam from the great ship gripped *Heart Light*'s hull and grappled with the opposing forces, trying to pull the hull back down towards the heaving sea.

Inside *Heart Light* we could 'feel' the dark forces fight against the beam coming from the hovering craft as we balanced precariously upon one hull. Slowly, the yacht began to dip her hull toward the sea but then, with a lurch, up she went again. *Heart Light* shuddered under the threat of being torn apart in this life-and-death struggle.

The Ethereans are known throughout the universe, but it has been so long since these great forces have manifested themselves in a dense third-dimensional world that they have become myths passed down through eons of generations from planet to planet, in the same way that the teachings of gods have been passed down through various cultures on Earth. These Seventh Realm beings have rarely been experienced, even in the fourth dimension, except at the moment of enlightenment. Their power is such that they are legends and icons, both worshipped and feared.

Throughout history, the Ethereans have been linked to Armageddon, the great deluge, the final decisive battle between the forces of good and evil, and the last judgement. For personal gain, political forces on our planet have manipulated the circumstances surrounding this event so that it has been misperceived by the human race.

The Ethereans represent the expansion of the Father of Primordial Radiation from which all consciousness springs, BRIH. They are one in the same thing, the Ethereans being but one step down in their vibrational field. One is manifest; the other is unmanifest. The Ethereans are called upon for service only when an evolving planet, ready to 'birth' or 'shift' into a higher dimension of expression, is being so 'interfered' with that all other available forces from lower-dimensional fields have failed to correct the situation. This is the case with Gaia (Earth) and her children.

Many forces have been sent in manifested form with the power of the *Christ* frequency: Jesus, Buddha, Zoroaster, Krishna, Mohammed, some eastern gurus, Jehovah and a few channels, to name just a few. But all have been undermined by a myriad of false prophets sent to cleverly confuse. If we are confused, we cannot make a decision. Our discernment becomes lost in the chaotic profusion of half-truths and arguments that purloin our very heritage.

Many have falsified the messages of the Great Souls in order to anaesthetize and manipulate the masses. The inhabitants of Earth are being groomed for a 'New World Religion' synonymous with 'The New World Order'. A *new messiah* will emerge from a fiery chariot, a spacecraft.

The interference has been dealt with through love, patience, power, deluge and destruction of its atomic matter, only to be amassed and manifested back into delusion. Nothing has stopped or slowed the consciousness of these deluded life forms bent on domination of the lower kingdoms. They have created a *time loop* in consciousness that has caught Earth's (Gaia's) inhabitants like flies cocooned in a spider's web. That time loop must now be broken!

The energy fields of Ethereans are unadulterated and their consciousnesses so absolute that the presence of just one outside the protective shield of its spacecraft amplifies a hundred times the power of the creative manifestation of any conscious being within its field. It was decided to bring the frequency of the highest manifested form of Primordial Source into our universal energy fields. This would permeate throughout the known and unknown universes, giving each and every living sentient being the power of unlimited manifestation through the opening of their seventh brain.

This would be devastating to any cognizant being with

an impure heart, no matter what tapes they play in their mind or words they profess to be their truth. Creative manifestation does not come solely from the mind, but also from the heart, where all conscious and unconscious desires lie. The risk is that this step is premature in human development. When the *quickening* reaches its peak potential, whatever lies within each and every individual's heart will *instantly* manifest.

The time for self-processing, self-development, addictions, dependence and enslavement is *over*. We cannot escape it by death for death is an illusion. This will be the greatest opportunity each individual and the whole of humanity will ever have to save themselves and the frequency bands known as *Tactile Manifested Reality*.

Heart Light is our wake-up call. The Seventh Seal is opening and spilling its frequency into the morphogenic fields on all dimensional levels. Consciousness is a constant ever-changing, emerging property. No one and nothing will escape the 'quickening power' of the Seventh Seal. We have been a co-creator with God and, for an instant, we will *be* God. In that moment, it will be an unclouded act of 'self-judgement'.

The only preparation we need is to look deeply into our own hearts and see what is crystallizing there — for there, and only there, will we find our next paradigm. The Ethereans are almost transparent in their appearance, for they are the *manifestation* of consciousness in its purest form. The *true* Ethereans are not to be confused with the much lower life forms called 'Zeta Reticulum'. These lower forms have been erroneously called Ethereans.

Etherean ships are advancing from ethereal spheres on frequency bands much higher than the third dimension. During certain 'time cycles' they can enter the Earth's denser strata and manifest into the corporeal world.

Powered by the 'elements', these ships traverse the heavens and the firmament between the luminaries beyond the sun and our dimension, skirting vortices, currents and vast whirlpools of energies.

The inter-dimensional craft that held *Heart Light*'s destiny in its grip had not yet fully manifested itself into third-dimensional matter. However, this did not deflect the power of the beam it was now emitting towards *Heart Light*, as legions of other Etherean ships moved through the expanding vortex.

During this life-and-death struggle I thought about the indisputable meaning of Darryl's last I Ching reading:

'The waiting is over; the danger can no longer be averted. One falls into the pit and must yield to the inevitable. Everything seems to have been in vain. But precisely in this extremity things can take an unforeseen turn. Without a move on one's own part, there is outside intervention. At first one cannot be sure of its meaning: *is it rescue or is it destruction?* A person in this situation must keep his mind alert and not withdraw into himself with a sulky gesture or refusal, but must greet the new turn with respect. Even happy turns of fortune often come in a form that at first seems strange to us.'

Suddenly, with a resounding crash *Heart Light*, once again, landed right side up — drifting, but intact. The astral and fourth-dimensional forces determined to block the Etherean's entry could not withstand the power of the beam in which they were struggling. I watched as the diabolical aberrations were overwhelmed and forced to retreat back to their dark asylums.

Once again, Darryl quickly moved to the navigation

station. Both engines had stopped. During the struggle, sea water had been driven up *Heart Light*'s exhaust pipes and had reached the core of her engines, making them useless. He urgently tried to get one, then the other, started, but to no avail.

Heart Light was now surfing down a wave, her beam lying sideways to the fearsome seas. Darryl immediately lashed the wheel hard over to starboard so the boat would stay beam on to the seas and, hopefully, round up into the wind to keep her from racing out of control down the face of the steep waves.

Salt water had poured through the flexing port windows, shorting out all of the instruments including the precious single side-band radio. As Darryl continued to fuss with the instruments, I told the children to sit back down with me and form a circle. My darling Shane, who had been the epitome of strength, now sat across from me with his body shaking uncontrollably.

Holding his hand, I explained: 'You, my love, are absolutely courageous. However, all the little cells in your body are full of adrenalin. Your lower brain has released all of it automatically in case you needed it for "fight or flight". You must separate yourself from your brain/body function and not personalize it. You are not being swept up in fear; you are just having a normal physical experience dealing with crisis.'

Shane started to understand and become calmer, as did Shali.

As we held hands, I told them we were going to combine the power of our consciousness to create a powerful ball of white, gold, and silver light in the centre of our little circle. We were then to expand it out to surround *Heart Light*, encompassing her mast, the full length of the boat and her hulls in the water. I told them we were to visualize and verbalize *Heart Light* staying upright and the waves calming all around her.

Still in a semi-trance state, I was not communicating to them about what was happening in the atmosphere all around us. I started the affirmation with a prayer asking the benevolent 'forces that be' to bring us an early dawn to strengthen my loved ones' hearts. Uncannily, a grey light immediately started to surround the yacht.

Keeping Shali's and Shane's focus busy, we took turns leading the affirmation. As one got tired, the next would take over. More and more light began permeating through the darkness, giving everyone a feeling of peace and security.

Shane opened his eyes and said, 'Woo, that was quick or am I imagining it? Is that light outside?' It was 4:46 in the morning.

Darryl went out into the grey light, the first time he had been outside the cabin since the storm struck. The seas around *Heart Light* had mysteriously calmed to a mere 25 to 30 feet and the wind was now blowing a gentle breeze of 45 to 50 knots. Shane followed his dad outside, tied the EPIRB to the captain's chair and then activated it. The war was over and we had won. Little did we know, though, that the heartbreak was to about to begin.

Darryl later wrote:
'As the hull lifted in our third broach, everything went into slow motion. I thought, "This is it". Our final death struggle. I knew it was over. We were going to capsize and all that remained was a few seconds before we would be upside down and the sea would be engulfing my lungs.

'I heard my voice say, "I did my best". I felt totally at peace with the world. I knew that the only thing that counted now was how well I died. I felt myself move into surrender. If it was my time then I would go in peace and harmony.

'My eyes looked for my Diviana. My mind wondered: Would she blame me? Would she hate me? How would she feel about me now that I had actually brought her to a watery grave? I had put her son and all of the planetary work she was supposed to do in jeopardy. All this flashed before my mind as our hull lifted higher and higher. Any moment now we would be upside down.

'I found her eyes. My heart soared and filled with love and appreciation. For all I found in her eyes was her love and surrender to me in that moment. There was no judgement; only acceptance. Her eyes told me that, if I needed to go through this experience to find myself, then it meant nothing to her. She enveloped my being with the frequency of love and telepathically I received: "I love you, my love. I will always be yours. It makes no difference where you are in the universe or what you do. I will always be there for you!"

'In that instant I found true peace. I knew that I was loved. I knew no matter what I did, *I was loved*. There were no expectations or conditions. I knew I had finally looked into the eyes of unconditional love. Today, this is the experience I hold in my heart. Nothing else means anything. This was the most precious gift that I could receive. I finally experienced God's Love. And, in that frequency, I was ready for my transition. I welcomed it.'

UFO research started in earnest around 1948. This research has been denied for years by world governments who have just recently started to release their hidden files and lies, to the amazement of their constituents. The United States government is now being forced to, at least, try to couch the UFO problem in a manner that fits into our shifting cultural beliefs. They are aware that they are dealing with a technology that transcends all material reality and has not only physical, but psychic effects as well.

UFO sightings and contacts have inspired people to the possibilities of contact with cosmic forces. Many support groups are meeting all over the planet because of personal sightings and contacts with UFOs and their occupants. No longer can their reality be denied by those who would cover up their existence because the social impact has become too blatant.

Psychic phenomena and UFO experiences are becoming undeniably linked together. It has become apparent that para-physical and para-psychological events are in operation. More and more people all over the planet, from all walks of life, are now realizing and experiencing not only extra-terrestrial, but extra-dimensional events.

Every single great event or individual that has changed the course of people's thinking or affected their souls has come from the *unseen* world, from another dimension — the Lady of Fatima, Lourdes, channelling, numerous UFOs, the origins of religion, the Holy Ghost, Spirits from the spirit world, Jesus Christ, Immaculate Conception, Zen, Buddhism, Armageddon; and these are just a few of the examples.

Most cultures of antiquity have recorded histories of 'beings' or 'gods' from other worlds with vastly superior technologies. Alien beings descending to earth and interbreeding with humans has been chronicled, particularly in the Sanskrit Vedas and the Hebrew Tanach, the old testament of the Bible, and many other recognized works such as the Mayan Codex. While much of the evidence has been distorted or destroyed, the vastness of these recorded works from historians, aboriginal holy men, prophets and seers cannot be denied. We have what is left of their fragmented marks on stone, papyrus, and clay tablets. They can be found in virtually every country in the world, including New Zealand, where the Maori people are now bringing forward the teachings they had hitherto hidden from the Pakeha, the white culture.

The only major event that people themselves have ever created in this world to change their way of thinking and affect their own souls has been through their love for war. Even this we choose to do in the name of something from the unseen world — god.

UFOs are now taking the forefront affecting mankind's conscious outlooks. Spaceships come in many different sizes and shapes, and for different purposes. They have been reported to be saucer-shaped, globular, cylindrical, oval, and more. People experience them as lights in the heavens, a planet that is moving, a star, or a satellite. When experienced closer up, many misinterpret them as meteors. As these space craft move into and through the Earth's atmosphere, many of them change colours because of atmospheric conditions. Many have the option to be visible or invisible, appearing or disappearing at will.

As well as the Etherean ships, there are a host of spaceships from many different planets and dimensions. They are all tentatively watching and waiting throughout the atmospheres around the Earth, like Indians surrounding a fort. The ships themselves are not important. Who occupies them and their diverse motives for being here is our only concern. If they were after material resources, they would have made their presence known long ago and, with their superior technology, have simply taken what they wanted. *They are after a much greater treasure than material resources.*

Whether these gathering masses are in resonance with the Etherean legions or not, they are here in ever-increasing numbers! Millions of them are now entering this dimension, this universe and this Earth's plane. And they have ONE purpose and ONE message: 'The Seventh Seal is now being opened for all of mankind. The Kingdom of Heaven is near at hand.'

The understanding and the meaning of this message is ready to be passed on, if the world is interested, and if its denizens are willing to let go of all their preprogrammed concepts long enough to individually discern it. This is a message of preparation for coming events. It is not just a message for the third dimension, but for all dimensions and their inhabitants. We are all facing the *choice-less choice*. We are past the 'Great Awakening'. It is time for the 'Great Lesson and the New Paradigm'.

CHAPTER 12

*T*he *S*an *T*e *M*aru 18

SUNDAY 5 JUNE 1994

■ 5:54 am ■

An emotional Jon Cullen called the New Zealand National Rescue Control Centre to advise *Heart Light* was well overdue for her check-in time. He assured them that we would have checked in if we could have.

■ Approximately 6:15 am ■

Darryl had left the VHF radio on in the hope that it might still be working. All the instruments had been knocked out during our final broach, minutes after our last check-in with Keri Keri.

In the morning light, we could clearly see what was happening around us. It was as if we were in a clear cylinder looking out at the storm surrounding us. We could see mountainous white-capped waves in the distance, but somehow they largely dissipated themselves before reaching us. Surprisingly, we were sitting quite peacefully, beam to the 25-foot plus seas. Only an occasional blown spume reached the interior of the cockpit. The wind, now a steady 40 to 45 knots, was almost like a deafening silence in comparison to the previous cacophony.

Suddenly, from out of nowhere, came a melodious sound, seeming most unreal at first. It slowly grew louder and louder, and finally gained substance as an RNZAF Hercules, appeared overhead, like the Calvary sweeping over the horizon to our rescue. The only thing missing was an accompanying symphony.

Excitedly, we ran back outside waving our hands as they gallantly dipped their wings. Could this really be happening? It was so beautiful, so exhilarating. Then we heard their heavenly voices come over the air: '*Heart Light. Heart Light.* This is Hercules. Do you copy?' The VHF had survived the broach! That sight and that sound created a special feeling never to be forgotten; a feeling that was shared, I am sure, by all the people who survived this storm.

Darryl had assessed some of the damage and reported: 'Hercules. This is *Heart Light*. Welcome guys. We're glad to see you boys! Our engines are stuffed. Our props are wrapped in drogue lines. Our mainsail and jib lines are tangled, and we are taking water on in the port stern engine compartment. I have the bilge pump running trying to pump it out now, so until it is cleared I can't tell where the water is coming from. But I think the hull is fractured. I don't know how long my batteries will last. We are all A-okay; just a little bruised.'

The Hercules said they would be back to us in a few hours. They were looking for *Quartermaster* and *Sofia*. As we watched them disappear over the horizon, I felt my mind starting to become more and more body-conscious. My earthly presence started to activate itself once more, like waking from a very vivid dream.

■ 7:30 am ■

Shali went forward to her bed to rest. I sat at the helm and opened the window so that I could talk to Darryl while he and Shane were outside pumping the water out of the port compartments. Darryl discovered a three foot-long breach in the floor of the hull, through which water was pouring. The force of the struggle during our last broach had managed to tear *Heart Light*'s hull apart. They took a piece of thick soft linoleum and some underwater epoxy and immediately sealed the gaping wound.

Darryl then found that both of our main batteries had been thrown loose from their box, spilling acid into the port engine compartment. The gases from the acid had permeated the compartment, gagging Darryl and turning the area, we feared, into a potential bomb.

■ 8:45 am ■

The Hercules returned to make sure we were still okay. Darryl anxiously talked to the pilot about the battery acid spill. After contacting command headquarters, he confirmed 'we had a potential bomb' in the port hull. If a spark got near it, it could blow. They told Darryl he needed to be 'very careful' if he was going to attempt to clean it up.

Very cautiously, Darryl climbed back down into the

engine compartment with rubber gloves on to further survey the situation. To his horror, the invertor located next to the batteries had been filled with sea water and was shorting out and starting to heat up. There was no way to turn it off. The only thing to do was cut the wires leading to the batteries, a course of action that could easily create the dreaded 'spark'. This seemed like a not-so-funny 'cosmic joke'; Darryl had thought he had survived his personal crisis and passed all the tests!

Holding his breath, he held bolt cutters around the wire, closed his eyes and snipped the wire. The wire was severed. Still holding his breath, Darryl waited.

Breathing easier, he started to clean up the spilled acid. It seared through the gloves, burning his hands as he laboured to clear the sinister substance from the hull.

Thankful when the job was finally done, Darryl continued his investigation of any further damage that might have happened during the battle. He came through the cabin door to talk to me with a look of astonishment on his face.

'What happened?' I asked.

'You won't believe this,' he responded. 'If we hadn't lost our engines in the last broach, we might not have survived!'

'What do you mean?' I asked.

'I just inspected the hydraulic steering ram and found the nut holding the steering arm together was a 'half turn' from falling off. When that happened we would have lost all of our steering and, at the speed we were soaring down those waves, it would have been a disaster!' he explained.

Not only had *Heart Light* found her spot, she had done it just in the nick of time.

■ 10:05 am ■

The New Zealand National Rescue Coordination Centre received a message that the 180-foot, steel fishing vessel *San Te Maru 18*, skippered by Bruce White, was standing by to assist in any way they could.

■ 12:11 pm ■

This storm was far from being over for a lot of other yachts in our vicinity. A fourth EPIRB had been set off and a Hercules was trying to find it. It belonged to the Kiwi yacht, *Silver Shadow*, a 42-foot Craddock design skippered by Peter O'Neill from Wellington in New Zealand. She had been hit by a rogue wave that capsized them 150 degrees, collapsing the starboard spreader and instantly dismasting them. Shortly afterwards, a full 360 degree roll broke their steering and autopilot, as well as the skipper's shoulder. The life-raft had disappeared.

■ 12:19 pm ■

The crew of the American yacht *Mary T* checked in. They had two drogues out. They were still taking on water and had their bilge pumps running while manually working the other pumps. Everyone was still okay.

■ 1:30 pm ■

Rescue control centre suspected that another EPIRB signal had been set off in the area around *Heart Light* and

Quartermaster. Not long after, the Hercules monitoring the area located a life-raft containing an activated beacon and no occupants. They immediately started to search for people in the water, being later joined by an RNZAF Orion deployed from Fiji. The Orion crew described the conditions as 'diabolical'. At times they flew at 300 feet above the horizontal missiles, fighting visibility problems.

■ 5:38 pm ■

During a radar search, the Orion located the *San Te Maru 18* running with the storm in order to save their vessel. They were asked to assist in the rescue of *Heart Light* and *Silver Shadow*.

■ 6:00 pm ■

We were informed by a circling Orion that the *San Te Maru 18* was under way to assist us.

■ 6:04 pm ■

The *Mary T* reported they were getting low on power. They would use their strobe light in order for the Orion to locate her. Everyone was still okay.

■ 8:00 pm ■

While shuttling in the dark between yachts the Orion crew spotted a searchlight beam. They had stumbled on to the American yacht *Pilot*, skippered by East Coaster Greg Forbes. The sturdy Westsail 32 double-ender had been rolled 360 degrees twice, the second roll bending the mast in an S shape. Fortunately, they were able to cut the mast loose. Said skipper Greg Forbes: 'We didn't have a radio, a life-raft, or an EPIRB from the start and our hand-held VHF had died. The miracle of it all was that we spotted an Orion and managed to signal them with three parachute flares and our searchlight.

'It was just one of those storms that was beyond comprehension. The pictures in Adlard Coles' *Heavy Weather Sailing* paled compared to the seas out there. They were breaking over the boat every couple of minutes. As the open cockpit filled with water, it was like sitting in a bathtub.'

■ 8:30 pm ■

I was lying on my back on the settee under a large clear hatch trying to find a break in the cloud cover. I wanted to see the heavens. As the boat heaved, I suddenly saw this magical glowing orb just above us. It was the beautiful Etherean spacecraft that I had seen in my mind's eye during our last broach. Fully visible, it was now glowing a golden orange. I could feel the tears well up in my eyes. It was a confirmation, a salute that all was well, all was real. We were not alone and would never be again.

I wanted to wake Shali and Shane, but the ship only stayed visible briefly before simply disappearing. However, I could feel her presence surrounding and protecting us, as if she had merged and folded her frequency bands around us.

Earlier, during the last hours of daylight, Darryl and

Shane had deployed the para-anchor off the front of *Heart Light* to ensure that we would hold our position for the approaching *San Te Maru 18*. We needed to make sure we stayed as close as possible to our last given coordinates in case the batteries on our VHF and EPIRB ran out.

Everyone was experiencing total exhaustion. While Darryl was on the front deck deploying the para-anchor with Shane, he had slipped and fallen backwards, landing on his hip and head. He had been stunned. As I watched him sitting at the helm, he now seemed totally spaced out and numb as he waited for further communication on the *San Te Maru 18*'s estimated time of arrival.

Deploying the para-anchor made an enormous difference to *Heart Light*'s animation. Snared by two heavy ropes off her bow, she was no longer free to surf down the waves. The seas had become more confused, with not all the waves coming at us head-on. They were coming from all directions. Being held by the big parachute gave some of these breakers tremendous 'punch' power as they slammed into the side of *Heart Light*. With the anchor creating a strong resistance to movement, *Heart Light* resounded from blows to the windows and beam hulls. The blows were always uncomfortable and, at times, harrowing.

Water continued to pour between the flexing cabin walls and the window frames. When Darryl saw his first 'window flex', his eyes almost popped out of his head. 'What the hell! How long has that been going on?' he exploded. I just looked at him and unemotionally said, 'Since last night'.

This time was to be the most uncomfortable experience of the storm for me. I was becoming more and more body-conscious as evening wore on. I was no longer in the deep trance-like state of consciousness. I was becoming fully present and I wasn't enjoying the scenery, the noise, or the movement of the boat. I felt drained, exhausted and still too spun up to rest.

I knew we were safe, even if a window were to punch in. *Heart Light* had not really sustained any permanent damage during the storm. She was still sound and strong. Even if she was to take on water, she was a catamaran and would not sink. The Etherean ship would not allow *Heart Light* to capsize. The *San Te Maru 18* was closing in and the Orion crew were keeping vigilance.

After the para-anchor had been deployed, I had tried to shift the muck and debris inside to make pathways and to clear some of the broken glass. During this time, while walking through the cabin, Darryl had cut the bottom of his foot quite seriously. As Shali bandaged him up, they both had a good laugh, comparing his bump on the head, bruised hip and cut foot to her list of bruises, bumps and assorted aches and pains.

I had Shali sit on the floor to help me shift things around. She was still vomiting bile mixed with blood. I kept talking to her and making her laugh when possible. All she wanted to do was put her head down. She was still ill and in shock. To her chagrin, I kept her moving a little here and a little there. I knew we had to somehow get her off *Heart Light* and on to the *San Te Maru 18*, and I wanted her to keep mind and body active so she would be able to transfer in the morning.

Darryl and I had discussed our plans for the future and had decided we would not allow her to stay with us after we received the help we needed to get back under way. She needed to get to land and stability as soon as possible. We spoke to Shane about going with her, but he insisted he was going to stay with us and finish the journey.

■ 10:09 pm ■

The French naval ship *Jacques Cartier* rescued the crew of *Sofia*. They had been knocked down, rolled and dismasted, and the skylight hatch had gone. Conditions were so severe when the rescue ship arrived on the scene its crew could not see *Sofia* within 300 feet of them while searching with a huge spotlight.

Before abandoning his floating domicile, the skipper quickly scrawled a message on the mast: 'Thank you for being such a lovely lady. We'll be back for you.' Miraculously, six months later, *Sofia* was found waiting for that promise to come true. Soon after, she was united with her prophetic skipper.

■ 10:15 pm ■

I was still laying on the settee, my mind full of questions. Would we simply get assistance from the fishing-boat crew so we could continue on our way to Tonga or Fiji, depending on the winds? Would the fishing boat give us a tow line and tow us to the closest anchorage? Would we be able to find the necessary facilities to repair *Heart Light*?

The VHF radio abruptly interrupted my thoughts when the pilot from the Orion spoke to Captain White on the *San Te Maru 18*. For us to pick them up on the short-range radio meant they had to be within 30 miles or so. While listening to Captain White talking to the Orion, I began picking up a strong psychic link to the voice on the radio. I went over to the VHF to listen closer. I was receiving very strong feelings.

When they were finished, Darryl suggested I should

see if I could raise the fishing vessel on the radio. Captain White and I had our first encounter.

He was soft-spoken with a clean, clear voice and vibration. As I spoke to him, I felt that I knew this faceless voice on a very personal level. I asked him the questions that had only a few moments earlier plagued my mind. He said he would check into it for me and let me know when he arrived about midnight. I hung up the mike and pondered this new frequency entering into my life.

Monday 6 June 1994

■ A little after midnight ■

The seas had either started building again or the para-anchor made it seem like they had. In any event, the motion inside the boat had become comparable to riding a bucking bronco. It was uncomfortably obvious that, if we had used the para-anchor at the beginning of the storm, we would have definitely found an early watery grave.

The only relief we could find was to lie down. Darryl and I were still too exhausted and strung out to sleep as we lay waiting. All of a sudden the whole interior of the yacht lit up with a startlingly intense bright light. We jumped up and looked out the window to see the huge fishing vessel moving across our port stern, creating a creepy and eerie feeling as we watched in silence. The dark hulk, with its huge spotlight shining in our eyes, was moving closer and closer to the boat.

Then out of the silence the VHF crackled: '*Heart Light. Heart Light.* This is the *San Te Maru 18.* Do you copy?'

Darryl handed me the mike saying, 'You have the link. You talk to him.'

Taking the mike, I said, '*San Te Maru*. This is *Heart Light*. Come back.'

'This is Captain White. How you doing over there? Looks like you're getting a pretty uncomfortable ride.'

'Roger that. We've put a parachute anchor off the bow of the boat so we would stay put till you got here and it's creating havoc. But we're doing okay.'

We discussed his strategy for staying on the high side of us throughout the night, and he told us that he was also going to keep the spot light on us. His young crew had excitedly offered to take one-hour shifts for the duration of darkness, in case of an emergency, or lest we somehow broke free and slipped away from them.

Captain White told us that he had not yet been able to get an answer from Sanfords, the fishing company that owned the longliner, about whether or not he could take us in tow. I told Captain White that, if we couldn't free the props, we would really appreciate a tow. I also told him that we would be grateful for any effort he could give us, as *Heart Light* was everything we owned in the world and we had no insurance to back us up. We even said we would be more than happy to pay for the fuel and his crew's wages if that would help.

As we spoke, Captain White started to mirror back to me the resonance I was feeling with him. We started to talk freely with each other as if we were long-lost friends.

'Hey, what's your name?' he asked.

'You won't believe me,' I laughed.

'Come on, what's your name?'

'Storm. Storm is my name.'

In disbelief he asked, 'How do you spell that?'

'S-T-O-R-M,' I spelled out.

After a short pause, he said, 'My dog's name is Storm.'

Thinking he had a bizarre sense of humour, I chuckled, 'You're kidding!'

'No. No, I'm not. She's a beauty! She's a Rottweiler and she's a good girl.'

'Well, I don't think I would be much competition for her at the moment!' I sparked.

We laughed and I asked him what his name was.

'Bruce,' he responded.

I didn't feel under the circumstances that I should give him any Bruce jokes, so I told him that was a nice name as my mind raced to figure out the numerological value of his name.

For years my mind had worked everything through numbers and frequencies. Even though I was not a numerologist and had little study time involved with it, I ran every new name, town, country, address, phone number — everything — through my mind like a computer sorting out frequencies. Studying Einstein had taught me that everything in the universe breaks down to a mathematical equation. I became obsessed with trying to find myself and others through breaking everything into frequencies.

B-R-U-C-E: $2 + 9 + 3 + 3 + 5 = 22/4$. Very interesting I thought. My life path in numerology is a 22/4. Storm is also 22/4.

'What's your birth date?' I asked.

With a slight hesitation, but obviously keen to humour me, he replied, 'August 14, 1958.'

My mind raced again, adding up the month, the day and the year. The total was 18, and adding the 1 and 8 together equalled 9, a sacred number. My mind started remembering all the 18/9 frequencies I had stored at the time:

- The yacht's name *Heart Light*
- *Heart Light*'s hull number
- The *San Te Maru 18*
- Captain Bruce White's life path.

Each equalled 18/9.

In numerology, the number 'one' in 18 represents the line between Heaven and Earth, the creative power touching the Earth's plane. Number 'nine' represents higher law, completion and the universalist who reaches out to the multitudes, easing their burden through understanding, wisdom and compassion. Nines represent the stage in life where the drama unfolds. Number '18' represents dreaming, healing, activity, organization, change of the outward structure of things, final completion. Coincidence? You decide.

We talked on as two old mates until the wee hours and then signed off, with Bruce promising to contact us in the morning as soon as he heard from the Auckland company.

■ 3:00 am ■

Darryl had lain down on one side of the wrap-around settee and I had lain down on the other side. We had moved so that our heads were touching as we lay on the wet cushions in the dark bucking yacht. Shane had come forward and was sleeping — half-lying, half-sitting — on the small double-seater across from the settee. He was too uncomfortable being forward. The boat was being slammed down hard after rising high into the air as the huge waves rolled under, over and through us.

He and Shali were afraid the stateroom windows would be punched out and their room filled with water, especially since the storm covers had been ripped off. However, Shali still elected to stay in the cabin and ride it out on a wet soft mattress rather than a wet hard floor or seat in the cluttered main cabin. She later shared that this was a very frightening experience for her. She kept thinking the windows would give and she might be trapped inside the cabin and drown. But she was too sick and too tired to move.

As I lay on the couch, I began to receive what could only be described as an 'inner transmission'. As I listened, Darryl suddenly whispered, 'Diviana, can you hear it?' I was surprised to find, after checking in with him, that he too was receiving the same transmission!

We listened intently in the dark. I reached over my head for Darryl's hand as I started to weep uncontrollably. Then I heard Darryl start to cry. We pulled ourselves up to hold each other; to cry in each other's arms, too emotional at what we were hearing to speak.

We were told that we must leave *Heart Light* exactly where she was. *Heart Light* had found 'her spot'. She was now sitting over a submerged temple that had been built ages ago over a vortex on the continent known as 'The Great Pan'. While the Polynesian people knew this continent as 'The Land of Kuai', scholars would later name it 'Lemuria'.

The 65-pound multi-terminated crystal that I had loved and worked with for the last ten years had acted as a navigational tool for *Heart Light* to find her 'spot'. This crystal was to now be returned to the temple.

Heart Light and her crystal cargo were to be sunk at that exact location to act as a beacon for incoming Etherean ships and an exit for souls choosing to leave the Earth's frequency band. *Heart Light* was to be sacrificed as a platform, a foundation for the New Paradigm message from the Seventh Realm. People would be more inclined to listen and 'know' the truth if Darryl and I sent her to the bottom by our own hands. She was to become a living testimony; a constant reminder to Darryl and me of the work we had chosen to come and do on the blue-and-green planet called Gaia.

We couldn't stop sobbing. *Heart Light* had become a living thing in our minds. She wasn't fibreglass and wood to us, she was alive — as much a part of us as breathing. She had been our home, our refuge from a cold insensitive world, our love, our escape. She had forgiven all our ignorance for years and brought us safely across oceans to new lands. So many of my memories of joy were tied to *Heart Light*. She had fought so valiantly to save us during the storm. And now her reward was to be torn asunder and sent to the bottom of the sea. I couldn't bear the idea of her being destroyed and yet in my heart I knew we would follow our destiny.

Darryl tried to console me. He spoke as a reawakened Divine Being: 'You know she has to stay, Diviana. It's our destiny. She is our metamorphosis. She is likened to a second skin to us. We have to shed it in order to be our full potential.

'We have to take the message to the world. There are brothers and sisters out there who can't remember who they are or why they are here. They are lost in confusion and manipulation. They can no longer survive imprisoned by the insanity that has been created by the collective stream of human consciousness. They do not choose to live in a frequency band ruled by war gods and entities who will try to take their souls. They are waiting for us to bring them the spark that will kindle their remembrance so that they can create a New Paradigm.

'All the highest of the Earth's frequencies will not be

lost. *Heart Light* is the tonal frequency the world has been waiting for — you are the Seventh Seal — we must give her to them.'

I listened to his words in knowingness and surrendered my heart to my destiny and *Heart Light*'s fate. She would live forever in our and the world's consciousness. She would be the beacon to herald in the New Paradigm. Nothing would be lost.

CHAPTER 13

Rescue at Sea

Monday 6 June 1994

■ 4:13 am ■

The yacht *Wai Kiwi II* reported that she had been knocked down twice in 70- to 75-knot winds.

■ Sometime after *Heart Light*'s final broach ■

Sub-Lieutenant Andrew Saunderson was standing watch with his watch mate on the Royal New Zealand naval ship *Monowai* when they saw a white flash. This is what they recalled.

Andrew: 'We were looking forward and the sky just lit up very bright. Then suddenly all the decks lit up; there was just all this light all around us. I just assumed it was lightning, but it seemed to last quite some time.'

His watch mate, Tracy Kaio, added: 'It was raining and it was really dark — no stars, no moon. Then a flicker of light and I thought, oh maybe we're going to get some lightning because we were going into the storm, and then the sky just *lit up*. We could see for miles. It was really quite strange. I looked at the officer of the watch and said:

"I've never seen a flare that bright before." I mean, *it was really bright*. I thought, what is this? It was all green! It was just . . . it was like we were surrounded in green light. I said, "What is this?" And Andrew was obviously looking at the green light, too.'

When I later interviewed Andrew at the New Zealand naval base, I asked him what he thought he'd seen. He didn't seem to know how to respond. Nervously, he raised his hand, pointing his finger up towards the ceiling. I said, 'Could it have been a spacecraft?' His eyes darted to his commander, Larry Robins, who was sitting next to me, and he quickly responded, 'No.'

'Perhaps a meteorite?' I questioned. 'Yeah, maybe a meteorite,' he replied.

After seeing the immense light, they promptly woke Commander Robins to report what they had seen. The captain came up to the bridge and, after discussing it, realized that it couldn't have been a normal safety flare because it was not the normal colour of a flare. However, he elected to put a call out on the VHF radio anyway.

A voice came back out of the void saying: 'Yes, we're out here. We saw it as well". It was the yacht *Ramtha* that responded. She had not fired any flares, but she reported that she had been under the intense light. This is how the *Monowai* found *Ramtha*, a 38-foot Roger Simpson-designed catamaran.

The crew of the *Ramtha* told how, during the height of the storm, helplessly lying hove to, her decks suddenly lit up bright as day. Roughly 300 feet above them was a huge, luminous green sphere. They watched it, incredulously, as it slowly turned to white with tinges of orange.

During their interview, Robyn Forbes stated: 'Bill stuck his head out from the bridge cover and looked directly above us.'

Bill, quite excited, interrupted her, saying: 'Ya. I stuck my head out and looked directly above the boat. Directly over us and about 100 metres above us in light clouds was this great big ball of light. It was a glowing mass of glowing white light, with just a tinge of orange. I just wasn't ready to see what I saw. It seemed to last and last. Eventually, I had to stick my head back in to check my heading. I had to be more concerned in keeping the heading of the boat to keep us upright at that stage. However, my mind was trying to figure out just what the hell this thing was.'

Cutting back in, Robyn continued: 'We thought maybe it was a fireball, because I saw the green, but when he put his head out the green light turned to white and then I saw the little bits of orange, sort of thing and I said, "I've never seen anything like that before!"'

Ramtha's Australian skipper, Bill Forbes, is a retired commercial pilot who later stated: 'I've seen a lot of lightning because I fly and I see all different types of lightning, the whole works, and at close hand, but this was nothing like lightning.'

Ramtha then heard a voice come from out of the hair-raising night on the VHF radio, the skipper answered it, and the light disappeared.

Forbes asked to be taken off their catamaran at first light with his wife, Robyn. Their steering had broken and they had nearly capsized three times.

At daybreak the *Monowai* manoeuvred herself in range of *Ramtha* to try to take off the Forbes safely. The conditions would not allow a life-raft. The plan was to fire a line from the *Monowai* across to the yacht. Attached would be a couple of harnesses so that the Forbes could be dragged back through the rough seas to a waiting crane on the bow of the naval ship. Commander Robins of the

Monowai informed the couple that he could not salvage their yacht or guarantee their safety in the tricky rescue.

Both vessels were drifting quickly and the *Monowai* crew feared their 3900-ton ship would roll on the yacht. After four attempts and four hours, the Forbes finally got the harness on to the deck. They were supposed to have time to set themselves up and then signal the waiting seamen they were ready. Then they were to jump into the water to be pulled back to the *Monowai*.

However, before Robyn could get her part of the harness untwisted and properly fitted, they were unexpectedly jerked into the tumultuous seas. As the *Ramtha* suddenly ran away from the *Monowai*, slipping down the face of the immense seas, the safety line with Robyn and Bill attached was free-reeling like a fishing line with a big fish on the other end of it. The anxious seamen had prematurely jerked the unprepared survivors into the frothing seas before the line ran out.

Although she had a life-jacket on under the harness, Robyn disappeared beneath the waves. The harness was hopelessly twisted and kept her down as she was dragged over 300 feet under water before being brought up for life-giving oxygen.

Watching from the bridge with trepidation, had been Commander Robins. He had had to make an immediate decision and decided, in order to save the Forbes, he had to leave Robyn harnessed under the seas and bring her to the bridge of the *Monowai* as quickly as possible where waiting medics could 'pump her out if necessary'. Robyn later said: 'I was under the water saying to myself: "I am not going to drown. I am not going to drown." '

To a spontaneous cheer and endless round of applause, the couple were lifted on to the ship by crane. Euphoria took over the entire crew as Bill, Robyn and the rescue team were finally safely standing on the solid deck of the *Monowai*. The Forbes were given a hot shower, navy clothes, soup and a bed to sleep in. They left the abandoned yacht to fend for herself.

Days after the storm, another yacht spotted mysterious green lights flying through the air. The Orion sent to investigate a possible sighting of flares found the abandoned *Ramtha*, floating aimlessly like a lost child. They could find no other sign of anyone or anything that could have fired the cryptic 'green' flares.

In flying around the surrounding area calling for any yacht that might hear them on their VHF, the Orion was responded to first by the Kiwi yacht *Windora*, anchored at Minerva Reef. They would not be able to assist. Then the Orion was contacted by the New Zealand yacht *Waikiwi* (not to be confused with the *Wai Kiwi II*, skippered by John Hilburst and lost during the storm). Skippered by Paul Mabee, *Waikiwi* was heading north.

With the Orion guiding, the *Waikiwi* was able to get a tow line on to *Ramtha* and tow her to Tonga. With the exception of the steering problem, there was surprisingly minimal overall damage to the yacht.

I was later told how Bill and Robyn's excitement over the return of their floating home was short lived. Instead of returning the yacht, the skipper of the towing vessel claimed ocean salvage rights, sparking a thorough investigation into the laws of mid-ocean salvage.

Skipper Mabee offered to sell the *Ramtha* back to the Forbes for an 'exorbitant' amount of money. When Mabee found out the Forbes could not pay the outlandish fee, Bill and Robyn were informed by him they would also not be allowed to take their personal belongings off the yacht.

Regatta officials and members, who had made it safely

to Tonga, voiced their outrage. No one could believe this was happening. However, Paul Mabee was to prove to be relentless until the Tongan government intervened. A reasonable and affordable payment agreement was attained. *Ramtha* was returned to the Forbes and Mabee lost his opportunity to be 'the toast of the South Pacific'.

■ 7:00 am ■

The *Monowai* headed for *Pilot* and the skipper, Greg Forbes, and his wife, Barbara, were safely taken aboard before abandoning their yacht. (These Forbes were from the United States, and not related to the Australian Forbes on *Ramtha*.)

Later, Barbara emotionally shared the following splendid story: 'We started to get ready to go. Greg started to batten down all the hatches when he turned around and said, "Barbara, look at that rainbow!" There was this huge 180-degree rainbow with really vivid bright colours. As we both stood there watching it, this great white ship was lifted right up into the centre of it. It was the *Monowai* coming for us.'

The *Monowai* also lifted to safety the crew of *Silver Shadow*. Said skipper Peter O'Neill of their scary transfer: 'I thought we were going to be crushed against the side of the boat. It was a very hard decision to leave *Silver Shadow* out there.' The yacht's crew were full of praise for the crew of the *Monowai*, saying they were superb, putting their lives on the line.

Five months later, *Silver Shadow* was found washed up on a reef in Vanuatu, over 1200 miles from where she had been abandoned. After valiantly surviving on her own for the rest of the storm, she had been boarded and stripped before being cut loose to find her way to an unworthy ruin.

■ 8:10 am ■

Another EPIRB signal was detected by the NRCC. It belonged to the *Wai Kiwi II*, a 44-foot Les Rolfe design skippered by Kiwi John Hilhorst. The NRCC contacted the Norwegian bulk carrier *Nomadic Duchess*, which agreed to rescue the *Wai Kiwi II*'s crew and proceed to Panama.

John reported: 'The wind continued to rise 70 to 75 knots and an enormous number of cresting waves were bearing down on the boat. We were getting pooped regularly with seas crashing into the cockpit every five minutes. One massive wave stove in a cockpit locker and water began leaking into the boat. We were knocked flat. Then we did a full 360 with incredible violence, like being hit by a bulldozer doing 40 miles an hour.

'We were knee deep in water in the cabin and two port hatches had been smashed through. I set the EPIRB and inflated one of our two life-rafts and secured it alongside. It was blown to bits and eventually tore loose.

'The mast was thumping against the hull. We had lost our steering and the self-steering was damaged beyond use. We had lost all of our communications and all our electronics. We had no option but to wait and hope for assistance.

After the *Nomadic Duchess* took the survivors on board, it tried to take *Wai Kiwi II* in tow. Any flicker of hope was dashed, however, when the line snapped and the yacht was caught under the transom of the massive freighter and smashed to bits. 'We lost her there,' said a devastated John Hilhorst.

■ 8:45 am ■

Shane was still sleeping when he suddenly startled us by jumping into the air with his arms flailing in front of him, calling his Dad. 'You okay?' Darryl asked as he moved to him.

'I was dreaming and, when we had that last slam down from the para-anchor, my dream spilled over into reality. I thought we were back in the storm again!' Darryl reassured Shane that all was okay and that it was just *Heart Light* fighting against her restraints.

Darryl then contacted Captain White on the VHF to tell him of our plans to leave *Heart Light* where she was. However, before he could say anything, the captain was explaining that he couldn't tow us safely through the steep seas. When Darryl told him it didn't matter anyway, Bruce compassionately told us we could throw as much gear as we could up to the *San Te Maru* and the seamen would try to salvage it. The two men then discussed tactics for getting us off *Heart Light*. We were to contact the ship when we were ready to be transferred.

Throughout the early hours of the morning, Darryl and I had discussed the challenge of how in the world we were going to sink a cat. They are built not to sink! They do not sink like a monohull that carries tons of lead ballast.

We decided to get our stowed shotgun and fire as many rounds as necessary through *Heart Light*'s hulls. Shane and Darryl struggled to get to the buried weapon but, no matter how they tried, they could not recover the gun from its hiding place under the floors. The access under the bed was just wide enough to slide the gun under the wing decks. During the broaches, though, the gun had slid out of reach. They tried everything, but there was just no way to reach it. In the end, we realized this plan would probably not have been sufficient to get the job done properly anyway.

Time was short, what were we to do? My mind raced, looking at the limited possibilities. I knew that if 'this was to be so', then the cosmos must have a plan! The *San Te Maru* 18/9 and the captain with the 18/9 life path were waiting as I watched the big longline fishing vessel standing by 100 feet or so off *Heart Light*'s port. Then I knew. The *San Te Maru 18* and Captain Bruce White were there to fulfil *Heart Light*'s destiny.

I jumped to the radio: '*San Te Maru. San Te Maru.* This is *Heart Light*. Come back.'

'This is the *San Te Maru*. Good morning, Storm. I hear we're going to have company.'

'Yes,' I replied. 'But, Bruce, we have to talk about *Heart Light*.'

I had a problem. I didn't know if Bruce knew that it was 'his job' to put *Heart Light* down. I couldn't possibly trust to tell him what had happened throughout the storm and what we had received only a few hours before.

First, I tried logic: 'Bruce, you know if we leave *Heart Light* out here she could become a major shipping hazard. Someone could run into her in the dark and sink their boat. This is the main cruising grounds and a lot of boats are traversing this area. Maybe, we should sink her?'

'Ya, you're right. I think maybe the air force or navy come out and blow the boats up or something like that.'

He did not realize that *Heart Light* needed to go down in this exact location and it was only a matter of time before the tether ropes would let go, setting *Heart Light* adrift in the fast-moving seas.

Using my womanly prerogative, I turned to my next tactic — pleading: 'Bruce, the tether lines are fraying through fast and *Heart Light* will be set adrift. Some boat could come along and take her in tow or she could end up on a reef somewhere and everything I own is on this boat. My whole life, all my personal things, my books, my writings. I couldn't possibly leave her out here adrift for someone to just come along and confiscate. You can understand that can't you? Bruce, I need you to sink her.

'Woa! Wait a minute. I couldn't take the risk. This isn't my vessel. I could lose my job. I wouldn't consider risking this ship or my crew for that matter. I am sorry for the position you are in and I will try to help you in any way I can, but I can't risk this vessel,' he asserted.

Testing him I said, 'I understand, Bruce. We'll figure out a way ourselves. Have you got a shotgun or anything on board we might be able to blow some holes in her around her water-line?' I asked.

'No,' he said.

'Okay then, we'll have to blow her up. I have four very large full propane tanks on board. We'll start a fire in the cabin and leave the gas on. We'll set it so that we have enough time to get off and move away from her.'

'Storm, are you nuts or something? You could blow us all up! I want to help you, but I don't think this is such a good idea. Let me think about it and I'll get back to you.' Realizing how serious I was about this situation, he signed off.

Shane, Darryl, Shali and I grabbed some plastic garbage bags and started throwing clothes and instruments into them. When they were full, we grabbed the pillowcases off the bed and filled them too. Darryl unscrewed my precious Joseph Pavsek original paintings, carefully wrapped them in the wet duvets (comforters) off the beds and then secured them with tape. All the crystals were to stay; however, I carefully secured my precious crystal wands to save them. We would throw as much gear as possible up to the *San Te Maru*'s seamen before jumping ourselves.

Suddenly, there was a lurch. *Heart Light* had broken one of her tether lines. She was free on one side. Bruce had been concerned that, if *Heart Light* broke free, he might not be able to catch her as she ran away down the steep seas. She was now half free and the wind was still blowing a steady 45 to 50 knots, with the seas running 36 to 40 feet. Darryl knew he had to get everyone off the yacht quickly before the other line broke.

He sprang to the VHF to call Bruce. The batteries were dead. Then he remembered his new hand-held radio under the captain's seat but in his anxiety to retrieve it, he dropped it, and it wouldn't work. I felt panic. Where was the cosmic plan? Why wasn't Bruce cooperating? Where was the mystical force that would move his heart to 'his awaiting destiny'? We were rapidly facing the reality of *Heart Light* slipping away from her 'spot'. I felt anger and confusion, and I began to get agitated.

I started to yell irrationally at Darryl: 'You promised me you would sink this boat on this spot. Get the kids off now. I'm going to blow her up. I've got to do it before she slips away! You promised me!!!'

He grabbed the hand-held once again and jostled the batteries. The red light came on: '*San Te Maru. San Te Maru*. Bruce, you got a copy?'

Bruce came back and Darryl continued urgently: 'Bruce, the tether has broken on one side. We need to get off now, and Diviana's . . .'

I grabbed the radio from Darryl: 'Bruce, I'm not getting off this boat unless you agree to sink her. I mean it. I won't leave. I'll blow her up. I'm not leaving *Heart Light*!'

'Calm down. Calm down. I'll sink her,' came his reply.

Surprised, I asked, 'You promise? You have to give me your word, Bruce. Do you promise?'

'Yes, I give you my word,' he responded, now a bit emotional himself.

'I'm trusting you, Bruce. Here's Darryl, tell him what you want us to do.'

Bruce told Darryl that he was going to try and manoeuvre his vessel as close along the side of *Heart Light* as possible. By drifting down on us, both ships would have their beams sideways to the seas. This would hopefully allow the two vessels to drift together. It no longer mattered whether *Heart Light* was struck in the process. Darryl and Shane were to throw as much gear as possible up to the waiting crew and then, one by one, we were to take turns jumping as hard as we could to the nets hanging off the side of the boat, hoping the crew members would be able to catch us and pull us aboard. Fortunately for us, there was a cut-out section in the solid steel rail on the side of the fishing vessel's deck. This made the dangerous jump seem more reasonable, as the crew had a better chance of getting their hands on us before we slipped and got crushed between the two impacting vessels.

Darryl, thinking about the single thread now holding *Heart Light* in place, was urgently telling everyone to get ready when a vibrating sound drew our attention. It was crazy. My two-foot tall Swedish Wood Troll, which had been screwed down to a cabinet, was now vibrating back and forth. The fearsome-looking piece of art had been a part of my family for years and was given the job of protecting *Heart Light* when we weren't aboard. I had decided she needed to continue her vigilance by going to the bottom with *Heart Light*. She was obviously not about to become a Swedish *Sea* Troll as she eerily vibrated her complaint under her own power.

Darryl and I looked at each other in amazement. At this point, feeling anything was possible, Darryl said, 'I don't think she wants to be left here'. He literally ran for a screwdriver and tore the cabinet apart to get at the screw underneath. He then placed the Troll in a heavy, but only half-full pillowcase, tied it shut and set it next to the padded paintings just inside the cabin door.

As the huge fishing vessel started drifting towards us, we looked at the rolling steel hulk with respect. We could see her bottom paint and the huge propellers churning up the seas as she heeled over. It was evident that this giant monolith could easily roll over and crush us beneath her giant superstructure. Captain White's skills became obvious as he worked the controls and manoeuvred the *San Te Maru 18* into place. His biggest worry was the rolling motion of the two vessels side by side. If anyone mistimed their jump and missed the nets they would be instantly crushed between the two hulls.

The *San Te Maru 18* moved closer and closer to *Heart Light* when all of a sudden her other tether line gave way. *Heart Light* precariously slipped away from the approaching hulk, turning her stern to the *San Te Maru* and angrily bashing into the steel ship with her steel davits, as if to say, 'Back off!' Darryl immediately reported to Captain White what had happened.

Then a miracle happened that would not be soon forgotten by the astounded onlookers. The seas and the winds temporarily abated as the clouds broke over us, allowing the sun to shine through. The heaving *Heart Light* stood her ground in her 'spot' as if caught in an invisible beam. During the entire rescue operation she lay within a tight circumference of where she had been tethered as the waves rolled under her.

Darryl and Shane quickly tossed the baggage up to the

waiting crew. Then Darryl told Shali to get ready to jump. We all held our breath as she stepped up to the opening in the stanchions and waited for what she felt was the right time to jump. The waiting seamen called to her trying to reassure her. Then she leapt for the side of the heaving fishing vessel. She was a little short and started to go down when three courageous fishermen lunged forward, capturing the precious cargo by her outstretched hands and arms. Next, they had her by her shoulders and quickly pulled her aboard to safety.

I watched, not relishing having to be the next one in line. I stepped up to the stanchion. *Heart Light* slipped backwards from the waiting seamen, as if she was reluctant to let me leave her. Hanging on to the sides, I moved forward about 20 feet down the deck towards the opening on the fishing vessel where the anxious seamen were waiting. Excitedly, they all started to yell at me, 'Jump! jump!' But that would have meant having to dangerously manoeuvre myself over the stanchion rails. Assessing the situation, I felt *the familiar calm* come over me. I looked into their alarmed eyes, raised my hands and called: 'Wait, just wait!'

I turned and walked quietly away from them, back to the opening in the stanchion near *Heart Light*'s stern as they anxiously watched, frustrated. Suddenly, with an enormous surge, a huge wave rolled from behind *Heart Light*, raising her higher and higher into the air and lifting her above the opening in the side of the fishing vessel. As she came down, the boats smoothly came together, almost touching. I took the hand of one of the mystified seamen and stepped gracefully on to the waiting ship. Smiling, I praised the boys, 'Good catch, eh?' I had arrived with all the aplomb and poise of a debutant.

Shane jumped to the nets and was pulled aboard.

Darryl had become so focused and concerned on what was taking place that, when the fishermen started to yell at him to jump, he completely forgot my beautiful Pavsek paintings and the pillowcase with the Wood Troll.

As if still tethered, *Heart Light* stayed very close to her 'spot'. It looked like she was surrendered and waiting for the inevitable.

Captain Bruce White would later relate the following about this event: 'When I was contacted and asked if I could assist with the rescue of distressed boats north of our position, I had this overwhelming emotion come over me. I started to feel tears come up and I didn't know why I felt so emotional; that wasn't a normal reaction for me. And then it was like something came *down* over the top of me and I calmed right down.

'We headed north nine or ten miles towards the stricken vessels and then we turned around and tried to go back, but the swell that was building just started battering us to the point that one of the boys, young Dan, said, "We're going to commit suicide. This is madness." We were being forced to turn back to the north towards *Heart Light*.

'It was getting on to about six or seven o'clock Saturday night. We weighed 364 tons, and within two hours of beautiful blue skies and calm seas we were in a life-threatening position. It all happened very quickly. As the night progressed it got more violent. We had water coming in under the bridge door and it is easily 20 to 25 feet off the water-line. The wind was howling that hard; I mean the wind was screaming! There were points during Sunday afternoon, where we couldn't see our rigging.

'There were times when our 183-foot vessel was surfing down the face of a wave and, as it came up behind us, it lifted us up. I've been in force 10 storms before, but

I have never been in conditions like that. I'm not saying the waves were 183 feet high, but they were stacking and we were surfing down them. I've been in a cyclone before and never experienced that kind of ferocity of wind and water. Any mistake and we would have been history.

'We were contacted by an Orion plane that had picked us up on their radar and asked if we would assist a yacht called *Heart Light*. We were already heading in their direction. Then we were contacted again and asked to rescue the yacht *Silver Shadow* and another yacht 13 miles away from us. I had to weigh a lot of things in my mind.

'I strongly felt that we were not going to be allowed to do anything but head for *Heart Light*. It was like there was this driving force — "we were going that way" — period! We had some 50-odd miles to run to get to *Heart Light*. I didn't feel I had an option. I headed for *Heart Light*. Later I found out, as if tracking her, we had set the same course *Heart Light* had taken throughout the storm.

'Later that night, we heard the Orion talking to Darryl, but he sounded real scratchy and broken up. I had difficulty dialling him in when suddenly Storm came on the air and she was clear as a bell! As soon as I heard her voice I felt real happy inside. I don't talk to people like I talked to Storm that night and I don't think I was doing it to make her feel better for what she was going through. It was just that this connection was there. The boys on the bridge deck all commented on it to me.

'When I arrived off *Heart Light*'s port, the storm suddenly eased — to me it just changed; if it hadn't I wouldn't have been able to sit off *Heart Light*'s port side like I did. When we first got there we were coming down wind, getting closer to *Heart Light*. I was thinking shit, we can't do this. We can't sit beside her in these conditions;

we're going to get *pounded*. But, as we came closer to her, the seas changed, especially the next morning when we were taking everyone off *Heart Light*. I'll never forget how Storm stepped aboard. I was thinking, "what's going on here?" I couldn't believe it.

'Waiting for daybreak, we just sat in one place for over three hours and didn't move. I got to sleep really well for the first time in two days. I didn't have to battle anything all night. It wasn't until after we had secured everyone on board that the seas and wind blew up again. It was crazy.

'After we were sitting off *Heart Light*'s port, no one wanted to go to bed. I had to tell the crew to go. But I gave everyone a one-hour turn holding the big spotlight on *Heart Light*. At daybreak, when we first really saw *Heart Light*, I couldn't believe what I was seeing. I thought: "They don't need us. This boat is mint." I thought we were going to find a boat one hull down and wallowing around in the water. That was the picture I had in my mind. So when I saw the boat, I thought, "What's wrong with this boat? There's nothing wrong with it. What's going on?"

'Then when I talked to Storm in the morning, she wouldn't get off the boat; she was blowing my mind. I told the boys, "Do you believe it? The bitch won't get off the boat!" I could see poor Darryl shaking his head. I figured he was trying to tell her, "We gotta go. We can't stay here anymore". Then he called me and told me Storm wouldn't leave and was telling everyone else to leave; that she was gonna stay and sink the boat.

I started to discuss it with Jim, my engineer. He had at one time sunk a boat himself. And he was telling me about the difficulties. Again this calmness had come over me and I felt it from head to toe through the whole thing. I didn't want to do it, but I knew in my heart I had to do it.

When Storm came on the air the last time, I said, "Okay, that's what we are going to do; now get off the fucking boat". We had made the agreement and I knew that's what we were going to do.'

Chapter 14

*C*auac:
*T*he *O*mega

Monday 6 June 1994

■ Approximately 9:15 am ■

Shali, Darryl and I were taken to the lounge area of *San Te Maru 18* to wait. 'Bosie', the cook, checked us for any medical needs and brought us various salves and creams for our cuts and bruises. Shane had stayed with the crew on the lower outer deck where our gear had been tossed. Later, he moved to the bridge beside Captain White.

It felt very strange sitting in this spartan steel-walled room with little round portals and its big metal table and wooden benches. Shali, Darryl and I sat on one side and Bosie sat on the other, staring at us as if we were the 'catch of the day'. Little was said and we had no idea what we were supposed to do except sit there. It felt like no one really knew what else to do.

Suddenly, I felt the big vessel lurch slightly as if hitting something. I instantly felt nauseous, knowing that Bruce had just struck *Heart Light* with the big ship. We sat there staring into space. I began to feel numb, as the *San Te Maru* lurched again.

Darryl got up and went to the portal and peered out at the sickening sight. There was a long deep gash running down the side of his beloved *Heart Light*. She was starting to list as the *San Te Maru* moved on her again, smashing through her port hull. Still, she held her ground. She was built like a tank and she would not give up easily.

As if time were once again suspended, the *San Te Maru* struck the fighting *Heart Light* again and again, fracturing her hull. Her upper coach house now had gaping wounds as the skilled demolition skipper relentlessly did the job at hand.

Bruce would later state: 'She just didn't want to go down. I didn't want to do it. She was a beautiful yacht. Where I come from and what I do made it very difficult, like shooting your dog. I started to get angry because it was taking so long. I just didn't want to hit her anymore; I just couldn't. But Shane was standing next to me and he said, "She wants it done; you promised." I told him, "Ya, but I don't like doing this. She wouldn't come up here and claw me or anything would she?" In the end, I got the job done.'

Shane would write: 'The only thing I have to say about this is, when I saw her being run over to sink her, it broke my heart. I talked to her, telling her it was okay; to give up now. It was time to go. But she wouldn't go! She was and is a true warrior, a warrior that was birthed from our consciousness and our creation. Finally, I said goodbye to her once and for all.'

I could not see *Heart Light* from where I was sitting and could no longer sit at the table with Darryl looking out the portal. I felt I wasn't being fair to *Heart Light*. I felt like I was being a coward by not being there with her when she went. I got up and went to the portal. All I could see were her two beautiful green bottom hulls shining in the light. She had capsized and was slowly starting to drift beneath the waves. My heart stopped as I whispered, 'Goodbye girl. I love you.' I felt a part of my mind, body, and spirit leave me as I watched her slip beneath the sea.

She was gone. I sat back down at the table next to Shali. I could see her heart break for me. She put her arms around me as I wept inconsolably. Still in shock, still sick, she had no idea of what had taken place over the last 36 hours except for hearing strange voices coming from the storm.

Time lingered on. We were getting uncomfortable sitting for so long on the wooden benches. All I wanted to do was find a bed and crawl into a long deep hole and stay there for the rest of my life. Bosie told us they were preparing a cabin for us and we were waiting for the captain.

It seemed as if we had sat there forever when, finally, a face appeared to fill in the gap of the previously faceless Kiwi Captain White. 'My comrade in arms' turned out to be a young man of 36, and slight of build with deep penetrating blue eyes that would not meet mine. He was quite attractive with his soft features and prematurely silver-white hair. He sat across from us and spoke only to Darryl. I thought this very strange. He would not look at me nor would he speak to me. I sat in silence and listened to them make their small talk and pleasantries of welcome, and then he left.

Bruce would later say: 'When it was done, I knew I had to go and talk to the waiting group downstairs. But something inside me kept saying, "You don't want to go down there; you just don't want to go down there". I felt very apprehensive, but I knew it was my duty because of who I was. I had to go down and talk to them.

'I couldn't look at Storm. I had no problem with Shane, Shali or Darryl. But I just couldn't look at Storm, for some reason I just couldn't do that.

'Later, it was okay. After we made the initial contact I felt okay; my fears went away and I was able to relax. The strange thing was, my fear had nothing to do with my sinking *Heart Light*. I had a lot of experiences as a child of feeling like I never belonged to my family; things that I could not explain and no one else could. As the days and nights wore on, with Storm being on the bridge most of the time, I realized that I had found somebody who could explain who or what I am. I felt that Storm, Diviana, knew the answers to all of it.'

Later, as Bruce, Darryl and I stood together on the bridge, we agreed not to tell anyone anything other than *Heart Light* had broken up during the rescue attempt and sunk. We knew the crew had photographed the entire incident. Later, they would graciously send us copies of the prints.

■ Approximately 10:00 am ■

We were taken to three small cabins approximately six feet by six feet square. There was a top and a lower bunk and very little space for two people to stand with the door shut. Darryl helped me on to the top bunk. I knew that Japanese people were short and narrow, but this was ridiculous.

I am five feet six inches tall and weigh approximately 120 pounds, yet my head touched one wall and my feet touched the other. There was not quite enough room in the width of the bunk to turn on my side and curl up. My shoulders were touching both sides of the bunk. It was like being packed in a sardine can. I wondered how the large Kiwi seamen were able to fit into these tiny cavities.

I didn't want to be a pest, but I became claustrophobic and just couldn't lie in the narrow cavern. We were moved to another cabin the same size, where I learned how the present crew were dealing with the Japanese-built narrow bunks. They had removed the side piece of the upper bunk and extended it out another three feet with plywood. This gave a good-size sleeping surface but took up most of the room in the cabin. Darryl and I shared this three-quarter berth for seven days. I was so deeply bruised, I could not manoeuvre myself into or out of the bunk without his help.

When we had abandoned *Heart Light*, we had opened up all of her windows and hatches, and latched her rear cabin door open. We wanted to make sure she wouldn't have any air pockets to prevent her sinking.

Shortly after Captain White reported that he had us safely on board, the *San Te Maru 18* was asked to hold its present location until receiving coordinates of a life-raft with an activated EPIRB. The *San Te Maru* was to intercept the life-raft and its contents and bring them back to New Zealand for inspection. So the *San Te Maru* then proceeded to steam in a circle around the sunken *Heart Light*, giving the crew an opportunity to collect flotsam from the sunken yacht.

I was lying in my bunk when Darryl walked through the door. 'I can't believe this,' he said. 'When the boys got the boat hooks out and went to the sea door to look for flotsam, this was banging up against the side of the *San Te Maru*'s hull directly under the sea window.' He handed me a dripping wet Swedish Wood/Sea Troll!

'How did she get out of the heavy bag, after you tied it shut?' I asked.

'I don't have a clue. I told you she didn't want to be left behind!'

When Darryl left the room, I held her in my arms like a child and softly wept. Would the tears ever stop?

Too hurt and spun up, I couldn't lie on the bunk any longer. I leaned over, pushed the door open and waited for someone to come down the narrow corridor outside the cabin. My beloved son appeared on the scene. 'How you doing, Mom?' he asked.

I told him I couldn't stay in there; I wanted to go outside. He helped me down and then hung on to me as we struggled outside against the motion of the longliner's narrow rolling hull. The storm had mercilessly blown up again. 'God, get a cat' was my only thought as we fell from side to side against the corridor walls.

Once outside, I watched the excited crew members as they used the gaffe hook to snare treasures. Shali's beloved teddy bear came aboard dripping wet and was put in the ship's dryer and then in the awaiting arms of this sweet little angel, too sick to get out of her bunk and join in the game the boys were having at the sea door. I heard Shane curse under his breath as the recently built, heavy and large cockpit table floated by. He had spent hours sanding and varnishing this beautiful piece of mahogany. Then came the rubber dinghy without its floor boards. One by one, shoes (none that matched), pillows, small cushions, books, albums, an exercise bag and bumpers were gaffed aboard.

I went back to my cabin; the sight was too painful. I felt heart-sick. I tried to hold the vision of what was to come from this disheartening experience, but at that moment all I could feel was pain and loss. As I lay on the bed, I saw, in my mind's eye, one of my Pavsek paintings. It was still wrapped in the duvet and floating within a reasonable

Heart Light's original logo artwork showing a lightning bolt through a heart.

Fueling to leave New Zealand on Tuesday 31 May 1994.

Heart Light off Bora Bora.

Heart Light's new logo and name decals.

The *San Te Maru 18*.

From the bridge of the *San Te Maru 18*, 4 June 1994.

Ramtha's Bill and Robyn Forbes being dragged to the *Monowai* on the tether; one of the very few times that Robyn managed to roll to the surface for a breath of air.

Top: *Heart Light*, as taken by a *San Te Maru* crew member.

Left: The *San Te Maru 18* battering *Heart Light*.

Heart Light's brave resistance is nearly at an end.

Goodbye girl. I love you.

The Swedish Wood/*Sea* Troll after rescue.

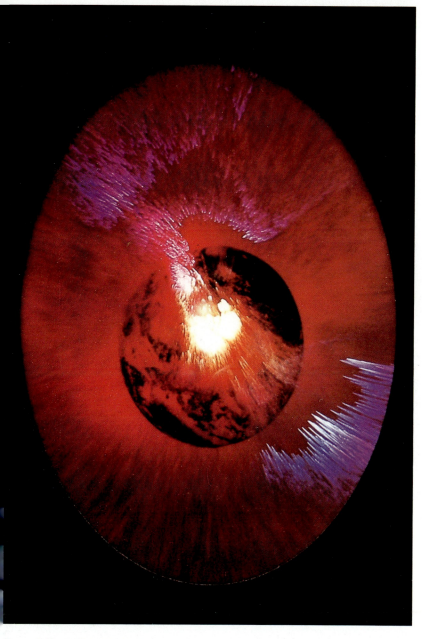

Joseph Pavsek's 'Vortex'.

Darryl and Diviana, 2 February 1995.

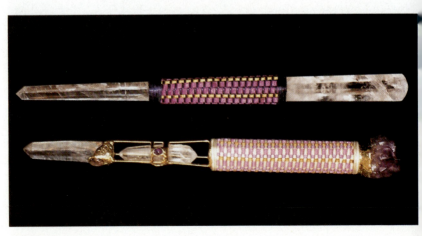

The repaired stalactite crystal (top) and the Ascension Wand.

distance of the *San Te Maru*. I called out for someone to come. A crewman appeared in the doorway. 'Get my son or Darryl, quickly please,' I begged him.

A concerned Darryl appeared in the doorway. After I told him of my vision, he immediately went to the sea door to tell the flotsam fishermen. Then he told Captain White what we were looking for. An earnest scouring of the surrounding area started.

Within minutes, one of the crew spotted the duvet-covered artwork. Excitedly, he called out directions and the *San Te Maru* steamed towards the painting. Carefully gaffing it, the trophy was safely brought aboard. My young sea champion would not allow anyone to touch it after it had been unwrapped. He had hooked it and he would deliver it. I stared into the beautiful painting. The soaked backing paper had fallen away. For the first time, I saw the artist had scrawled its name: 'Vortex'!

We steamed in circles around the area for about an hour and a half before Captain White received the coordinates of the life-raft, approximately 23 miles away. Two hours later, as we approached the rendezvous point, Darryl came to the cabin and asked me if I wished to be on deck when they encountered it. I struggled back up top to watch.

Suddenly, this rapidly moving object appeared, free-falling down the face of a 30-foot swell. The thing that struck all of us was the speed with which it was travelling as it skipped and bounced down the steep waves. I thought, 'My God, no one could survive in that thing and that motion. I'd rather be dead!'

With his systematic skill, Captain White brought the *San Te Maru 18* around so that the flying passengerless life-raft met his vessel directly under the sea door, where the waiting crew gaffed it and brought it on board. It was a harrowing sight. I knew immediately that it belonged to *Quartermaster* and not *Silver Shadow*, which had also lost a life-raft during a roll in the vicinity. Even though there were no identifying marks, I remembered this raft from my earlier vision of *Quartermaster* and her crew.

Not only was the pink canopy shredded and flapping wildly in the wind, but a large portion of it had been torn away. The painter (rope) was still connected to a stainless-steel hook that, in turn, was connected to ripped wood and fibreglass. The painter was covered in red bottom paint, creating an undeniable mental picture.

The boys turned off the activated EPIRB and took it to Captain White on the bridge. Wellington later confirmed that we had, indeed, picked up the *Quartermaster*'s empty life-raft. It was generally suspected that someone had been inside at the time the life-raft had been torn loose during a roll. Survivors of this storm unanimously agreed that it would have been impossible to get into a life-raft in the conditions they faced.

Later that day I went to the bridge of the *San Te Maru 18* and discovered a single card from my Mayan Oracle deck (as written by Spilsbury and Bryner) sticking to the window in front of the helm. It had mysteriously attached itself to a gaffing hook while one of the boys was trying to spear a shoe out of the water. The card was one of 44 in a deck and was called Resolution of Duality. It challenges the holder's perception of duality, mass consciousness, personal resolution and the integration of polarity. Its presence made quite a stir amongst the superstitious crew and captain, who kept the card as a personal symbol.

The following morning I was awakened by Shane. Standing at the side of my bunk, he had just come back from the showers and was radiating a deep centred glow. I smiled at him lovingly: 'What's up?'

He looked at me with a 'new' profoundness: 'You know ever since my motorcycle accident in the military, I have never really gotten it totally together. I mean, my self-image has suffered a lot because of some of the stuff that happened to me.

'I know how hard you've worked with me about being defensive with new people, but I just felt I needed everyone else's approval to be okay. Well, I just want you to know that after what I've been through with you and Dad this last week, I don't need anybody's approval for anything — not ever. I know who I am now, Mom. I know that I'm okay just the way I am and that I am a pretty good person. I just wanted you to know. I promise, I'll never feel lesser than what I am again,' he said with a smile. 'I mean it.'

When Shane was 21 years old, he was in a very serious motorcycle accident and in hospital for over a year. He survived three major brain operations. This did not affect his intelligence; however it did affect his short-term memory. This, in turn, affected his ability to be able to quickly remember the words he was after to express himself.

He had always been a very different child growing up, and had to suffer ridicule when he was younger because we had raised him a vegetarian in a meat-eating world and a metaphysician in a materialistic world. His surgery compounded some of his feelings of being 'different' from others, which was a constant source of pain for this young man trying to find himself in an estranged world. My heart swelled with pride as he claimed his *gift* from the storm.

CHAPTER 15

*A*hau:
*T*he *A*lpha

FRIDAY 10 JUNE 1994

After five days homeward bound aboard the *San Te Maru 18*, we stood at the ship's rail to welcome the coast of New Zealand on the horizon. We had spent the better part of the week searching for fishing nets, beacons, and gear the fishing vessel had lost during the storm. After an extensive search all we were able to recover was one of the activated beacons.

Although instructed by his company to continue fishing, a sympathetic Bruce decided to return to Auckland to unload his rescued cargo. As New Zealand drew nearer, Bruce was in direct radio contact with Sanfords. We were all quite concerned about our reception ashore, anticipating a swarm of media people.

As we stood on the bridge, the men joked about reporters and their relentlessly stupid questions. 'How did it *feel* to almost die and lose your boat?' they mimicked. We couldn't help but laugh when we at last stepped on to an Auckland wharf, only to have a television reporter thrust a microphone in our faces and ask that very question! What were we supposed to say? We elected to ignore him.

We made Darryl our spokesperson after agreeing earlier that he was to give only glowing reports of the *San Te Maru*'s talented captain and courageous crew. Approaching port, Bruce informed us that there had been a tremendous number of phone enquiries as to our estimated time of arrival. Shali became very excited and bubbled over, creating verbal pictures for us of her father, who would be at the head of the line on the dock, and what he was going to say to her and to Captain Darryl.

We knew her father had been very rigid in not giving approval for his Kiwi daughter to make the sea passage to Tonga with her new American family. Now in her thirties, she had spread her wings in defiance and chosen to seek adventure. And adventure she had surely found.

Coming into the sparkling waters of the beautiful Waitemata Harbour in Auckland, we were re-routed from the *San Te Maru*'s usual dock to a more secluded wharf to try to keep the media circus to a minimum.

Darryl and I were completely surprised when we docked. There were all these wonderful supportive people waiting for us. Some were from my spiritual classes over the years. Some Darryl had done marketing and consulting work for. Others were just concerned friends. Yet others we had never met were there because they 'had experienced personal psychic experiences about us and *Heart Light* during the storm'. They were eager to share and substantiate their dreams and visions of what had taken place on *Heart Light*!

Some brought clothing and warm jackets. It was all unexpected and greatly appreciated. We were not to worry about transportation or a roof over our heads; it had all been taken care of. We were just not prepared for the overwhelming and beautiful reception we received.

Feeling a bit foolish and embarrassed, Shali asked and looked everywhere for her father. He was not to be found. She knew he must be late in getting there and she would wait. My heart went out to her. She was still so pale and ill, and she longed to be held like a child in her beloved father's arms. He did not appear. Later that evening, when she called home, he sternly admonished her willfulness in leaving New Zealand against his wishes.

After a tearful night, Shali appeared in the morning. As Shane had done earlier on the *San Te Maru 18*, she was ready to claim her compensation from the storm. She told me: 'I've thought about it all night and I have come to the realization that, if I could survive that storm, I am strong enough to withstand anything and anyone — I can stand in my own light!' And she is.

A few days later she asked: 'When are we going cruising?'

'Soon, very soon,' I answered. 'But this time not by boat. This time through the cosmos!' As her face lit up, she replied: 'I'm ready.'

After a few days of rest, as I had promised everyone on the dock, we now sat in the lovely lounge of a friend's home with a very eager group. Darryl and I had decided that it would not further anything at that time to try and illustrate all of the events that took place during the storm. With this book gestating in me, we also chose not to do media and magazine interviews except to highlight events. However, this group of people was more switched on and connected than we had realized! We taped this session and the following are some of the experiences these advanced souls had during the storm.

Two mates, Ester and Julian, both school teachers, told us a very touching story as they placed a large round rainbow candle in front of us. It was about half burned down and had a piece of artwork that was used for letterhead taped around it. Darryl had sold this couple our computer before leaving and it still had all of *Heart Light*'s letterhead and logos on the hard drive. Ester and Julian had printed out the letterhead, and taped it to the candle.

Every night and morning of the storm they had lit the candle, called others in the group to synchronize with them, and then prayed and meditated in front of it, visualizing us safe. They stopped only when they heard we had been picked up by the *San Te Maru 18*.

Several of the people in the group had remarkable psychic experiences, describing quite graphically the dark energies surrounding *Heart Light*. Others saw monstrous seas. They had used all their will-power to calm the seas and white light the boat against the dark negative forces.

Pam, a business executive, told us that she had been magnetized by a genuine hawk talon while in a Wellington antique shop. It had been treated and placed in a silver jacket so that it could be worn on a chain if desired. It was quite large and sported a silver ring on its middle claw.

She said she was not sure why she bought it until, after the storm, she had been guided in a meditation to take it to Diviana. Producing the talon from her pocket, she said to me, 'I have been guided to tell you that you are to use the power of the hawk'. She then handed me the claw, saying that she knew that whatever was taking place was happening from a very high level.

I looked at the thing in my hand. It was not exactly aesthetically beautiful, but it did exude a quality of power in its representation. I then told the group a strange tale. During the week prior to leaving on *Heart Light*, I would hear the cries of a hawk just before I went to bed each night. Hearing such a sound so late is strange. Then, when I awakened to go to the bathroom in the night, the creature would immediately start calling as if it could see through the walls and drapes.

I didn't think too much about it until the third night. It went on for five straight nights and then on Friday morning, when I opened the French doors to the garden directly under my bedroom windows, there was a very large hawk feather lying at the door. I knew then it was an omen, but I didn't know what it meant. I took the feather and placed it in a shield hanging over my bed on *Heart Light*.

Another woman had brought a book with her that, coincidentally, if there is any such thing, had information about hawks. She read to us: 'In the "Shaman" tradition, the hawk represents a "Messenger from God".'

Next, a mystifying experience was related by Rex, a man I had never met before. Rex, a roofer by trade, was in his thirties and not particularly interested in new age, sci-fi, or anything out of the ordinary. However, he had this dream or vision — he wasn't sure which because it had been so real: 'It was the Sunday morning of the storm. In my vision I saw a yacht coming towards me. As the yacht came past me I could see the stern very clearly. It said *Heart Light*. Suddenly, like in a computer graphic, the yacht turned into a "spaceship", veered off and flew straight up. It was very, very large.

'I then saw three cone-shaped spirals that looked like they were made out of vapour or something. I looked up through them and saw fleets of spaceships coming down through them. I felt very exuberant! I didn't know where they were coming from or where they were going.'

So much for not telling the group about what

happened out there! Without going into too much detail, I confirmed Rex's vision. I don't think Rex will ever be the same again. I know we won't.

Then Marion, a woman I had met shortly before leaving New Zealand spoke. Marion was a lovely lady, also in her thirties. She told us a bit about her life and that she had lost a child and had had a near-death experience. After that she started having visions: 'For the last three years I have had dreams about Diviana,' she said. 'When I found out that a friend of mine was involved with her, I just knew I had to meet her. Shortly after, I did. During a meditation, I was shown that Diviana was birthed into this world of physicality, and into the earth's consciousness, to open the Seventh Seal.

'I never told Diviana and at no time has she ever conveyed to me who she is, but I knew she was to be responsible for the change in consciousness that was to come about through the opening of the seal. I know that this took place during the storm. She dared to go where no one had been at great personal risk. I want her to know that I know what took place out there.'

The room became very quiet. I looked at this woman in utter astonishment. For the first time since the storm, I felt that Darryl and I weren't alone in the task at hand. I knew that *Heart Light*'s story was just the beginning. That through any means necessary, I would herald the significance and meaning of this event and how it will affect every corporeal being. I smiled at Marion and nodded my head in appreciation; this was something that I chose not to discuss at the time.

Then Jaguar spoke. She was a fitness expert with a gorgeous body, and had been instrumental in helping her mate, Michael, successfully introduce the product Spirulina to New Zealand. 'I'm so glad you chose to stay!'

she started. 'I wasn't ready to say goodbye. During the storm, I was so concerned and emotional about what you must be going through. I wanted to feel and be close to you so I went into meditation. Then I pulled a card from my Mayan Oracle deck, asking it to help me understand what this experience meant for you.'

She laughed heartily. 'Guess what I pulled — your card — Cauac: Electric Blue Storm! I brought the oracle with me to read to the group today because I knew yours went down with *Heart Light* and I didn't know how many people here would know what I was talking about.'

Jaguar read: 'Cauac, Electric Blue Storm: It means Purification, Transformation, and Activation For Ascension.' Because it was a long reading, she then summarised, saying that the bearer of this frequency had the necessary energy to snap people from their trance and shatter the structure of their programmed reality. It was about 'going home' through freedom from vibrational density. She finished by reading: 'Cling not to this, or that, for nothing will remain after the "Storm" save the beauty and ecstasy . . . the perfect naked truth of who you are.'

Bruce, captain of the *San Te Maru 18*, then gave his own wonderful account of how *Heart Light* and the universe delivered Diviana on to the decks of his ship, amazing him and his crew.

I was starting to feel overwhelmed by all of it. The storm, the aftermath, and now all these beautiful souls sitting here, so open and waiting as if for a miracle in their lives. I began to be filled with a strength, a courage, and a commitment for the potential of what was to come.

While meditating a few days after the group sharing, I had a cognition of a group or persons doing a film on the storm rescue. I knew that I was somehow linked with the director or manager of this film and that he would be contacting me soon. As June and July moved on and I still had not been contacted, I started to wonder if I had been mistaken. Finally, one evening the phone rang: 'Hello. This is David Baldock from Ninox Films calling. Can I speak to Darryl or Diviana Wheeler?'

Without thinking, I replied: 'Well, it's about time. I've been waiting for you to call!'

'You have? How did you know?' came his surprised response, jarring me to my senses.

I apologized, made light of it and said that we would be quite happy to meet with him. We agreed to the following evening.

When we duly met, he had his entire film crew with him ready to do a recorded interview. Knowing that our interview might have a different hue to it than his previous interviews, I told him that I would have to get back to him about the time and place, and that I wished first to meet with him personally.

I felt uncomfortable at having so many people whom I had never met before coming into the little flat Darryl and I had rented on Lake Pupuke in Milford. It was in a gorgeous setting under a lovely home. However, I didn't have any furniture. We were using large Indian cushions to sit on the floor around a borrowed glass coffee table. The whole flat was strewn with little crystals and sparklies given to us as welcome-home gifts. It was quite comfortable in the interim, but certainly not the self-image we wanted to portray to a conservative local film crew, especially with the account we were about to give. I made arrangements with my landlord to meet with David and one of his people the following evening upstairs. It was an elegant home, reflecting the atmosphere of a very successful businessman.

David arrived with Shara, his production manager, promptly on time. He was a pleasant man in his early forties, with a soft mannerism emanating warmth and sincerity. Shara was a switched on young lady who was obviously considerate and very keen to do the interview. They both looked very tired. They had been all over the country, the United States and most of the Pacific Islands, tracking down every person who was either in or participated with the storm on some level. They were in Auckland to film the *Destiny* team and then off to Western Samoa to catch up with the *Monowai* and its crew.

David told us that he hadn't been able to find us and that another person, who was also writing a book about the storm, had informed him that we had left the country and gone back to the United States. This was the same person whom I had, a day or two earlier, granted a limited interview for his book. David had found us quite by accident. He had spoken to one of the Orion pilots who had met Darryl and me at a gathering at the home of the *Destiny* group. We both felt that fate had been kind and we found that we had a wonderful resonance with which to work. This pivotal meeting was to clearly become of paramount importance in supporting the events that took place on *Heart Light*.

After our initial meeting for an hour or so upstairs at my landlord's, we agreed to do the filming the night they arrived back in Auckland from Western Samoa. David then told us that his entire film crew were only a few blocks away, having a drink at the Mon Desir Hotel in Takapuna, and were all very anxious to meet us. We thanked our landlord for his hospitality and headed off to meet the waiting film crew.

A few minutes later we were sitting down with the crew, who looked as though they had been through the storm. I suppose that on many emotional levels they had, after listening intently and filming all the tragic personal stories of the people who had survived the horror.

David introduced us to Paul Everett, a close friend who was helping him with the 'Doco', as they called it. Paul sat there very quiet, at first not saying too much. He looked a little nervous. David explained that Paul had been on the yacht *Irresistible* when the storm hit, and it was because of Paul that David had decided to do the film. He said that Paul had come back from the storm a completely changed man, refusing to discuss what had gone on that had affected him so deeply. But he was quite keen to report on his yachting experiences during the storm. This seemed to deeply puzzle David, especially since the two of them were such great mates.

As the group chatted away, giving their impressions of this and that during their previous filming, I was able to draw Paul into a private conversation. He still seemed a little apprehensive. However, within a few minutes he started to communicate more freely, hesitantly telling me some of his experiences. Then he completely opened up, telling me about hearing strange foreign-sounding voices coming from out of the storm. He saw different apparitions during the electrical storm that had totally bewildered him. He went out to the film truck and brought me back his journal and told me that he had written his experiences down and that I could use any and all parts for my book if I would like.

He then told me a most unusual story, a story that would explain his nervousness upon meeting Darryl and me: 'I was on watch during the storm. I looked down towards the companionway. I looked again because I was sure I could see the image of two people just sitting there, like in a film being played in the darkness. There was no fear in these two people. I just couldn't work this out. All around me was mayhem and here, sitting in front of me, were these two people totally at peace and in harmony.

'I thought, no, I must be dreaming. I must be seeing things. But I could outline a man and a woman looking at each other. In a way it was very comforting to me to see how peaceful they were, just sitting there in front of me. I've got to stress that there was mayhem all around me and to see these energies; being so frightened this gave me a good feeling of warmth and security. When I saw you sitting together, a chill went up my spine because I knew it was you two I had seen during the storm. I have never told anyone about this. It's just too much of a coincidence. I've never met you guys before. You explain that one to me!'

David heard his friend tell me this incredible story, and looked quite astonished by it all. But he knew Paul was not the type of person to make up things, especially of this nature. I started to very carefully ask David questions about his other interviews. Had anyone else seen anything strange during the storm, like apparitions or strange lights? Had anyone else heard voices?

Suddenly, David sat straight up in his chair and blurted out, 'Oh my God, my God. I just never put it together! There was so much being said and taped, I just never put it all together!'

He proceeded to tell me first about the yacht *Ramtha*, then the naval ship *Monowai*. About how everyone that made it to the regatta headquarters in Tonga was talking about all these strange voices coming from out of the storm. He remembered others who were experiencing 'evil presences', 'apparitions', and on and on. The yacht *Arosa* had told him about bright flying lights up in the sky. The yacht *Southern Voyager* told some of the film crew to go and talk to one of their crew, who was in his sixties and had been hearing 'the voices'. Paul added: 'At the time, I immediately linked this in my mind and knew that I wasn't going crazy, and that there were other people out there who had heard these voices!'

After giving David our interview the following evening, he told me that he would collaborate with me in any way that he could to help me find and bring factual information from other people experiencing phenomena during the storm. Destiny was still at work, three months after the storm.

As David now interviewed more of the people who had taken part in the storm, he started to ask more decisive questions that could possibly support my account. For example, when he interviewed Greg Forbes from the yacht *Pilot*, he asked directly if he had had any unusual experiences. Had he seen anything, like strange lights or perhaps heard voices?

A reluctant Greg Forbes responded: 'I'm sure this was my own mind at work, but I heard — well, I listened to this monologue all through Saturday night, through the worst of it — sort of a mindless monologue between people. There were times when I actually thought that we had sailed by somebody that was out there, that I could be hearing these voices from. But it was just so erratic and senseless that I thought I must just be producing it myself.'

I would receive excited and enthusiastic calls from David in Wellington about his new discoveries. He once said it was like opening a package that had many layers of wrapping around it. He was wonderful as he tried so hard to stay open and objective about the whole situation, faithfully calling me to make sure that every detail was covered accurately.

When David had finished his Doco and sold it to the television networks, I had an interview with him. I began: 'This is Ninox Films. Today is December 5, 1994. I am talking to David Baldock, the managing director of Ninox Films. The reason I would like to do this interview is because I have written my book from a chronological and exacting level of all the events of this phenomenon. I have found that they are all tied into the same central core issue of what took place out there. Within this framework, what I am looking for is simply for you to express, in your own words, when and where you started to realize that you were dealing with something much more than just an immense storm and rescue operation. When did your "light bulb" switch on and how do you feel it has affected your Doco?'

'Well, I guess for a start, we are specialist documentary makers. When I realized that my close friend Paul Everett was in this storm I, of course, followed it very closely. However, it wasn't until after Paul got back and I started talking to him that I realized the immensity of what people had experienced out there. And this was before I realized that there was any kind of phenomenon taking place, because Paul was not telling me about that part of it. So just based upon the impact of the storm itself on his life, I felt that there was a story there that needed to be told.

'I managed to secure a small budget from one of the local television stations, but the story just kept growing and, when that budget was gone, I felt so strong about what I was doing, I started pouring my own money into it.'

I asked: 'During all these interviews you were having, people were telling you about hearing voices, seeing lights and so on, and yet you never connected any of it in your mind?'

'There were a lot of things I never picked up on. The guy on *Arosa* talking about amazing lights in the sky; an amazing phenomenon in the sky. I just thought he was talking about an awesome electrical storm. There was just so much, I just didn't connect it. However, after doing your interview, you brought another dimension to it. I started to think back and also, as I did further interviews, I started to ask questions that connected with your experience and that was when I realized that this film was starting to take on a life of its own. We began to realize that this film just had to happen. We were getting everyone that was involved now and getting the full picture. It came to me that this whole incident had far greater ramifications than just a New Zealand storm!

'I began to realize that there was something going on that I didn't have a clear answer for, and I still don't. I know that there are explanations that haven't come up yet. That is why I am fascinated to get to read your account — your book — when it is finished. However, it just keeps on going on. I keep seeing more things in it. Even now as I am looking at it, there are just more and more things that I can feed back to you and I know there will be more.

'This documentary is evolving still. I know, I just now remembered one of the things that sparked me. I was reading the *Evening Post* a while after the storm and it was just a wee piece that said an orange light had been seen at certain coordinates and the rescue centre didn't know if there could possibly be another yacht in trouble or what, so an Orion went to investigate it. There were no yachts anywhere in the vicinity to be responsible for this "orange light" and yet this is how they found the yacht *Ramtha*. So I thought people are not connecting all this stuff. They're not drawing all the dots together and it actually needs to be connected all together. What was that light? Where did it come from? So that is when I really started to know that there was *something* going on!

'I have a belief that this film is very important. You have such a wide band of people who looked death in the face. I feel this is a film that just will never stop. There is an ongoing element that just keeps growing out of this film! And in that sense this film has totally a life of its own.

'It has its own path and its own destiny. I have not had to go out and really push this as a product. This film, it — it just has an awareness that we haven't even created. It's coming from somewhere and people from all walks of life are waiting for it.'

After further conversation I told David of my fascination with numeral frequencies involving the storm. About all the nines, 18/9s and 22/4s surrounding *Heart Light*, me, Bruce and the *San Te Maru 18*.

As if stating a revelation, I said:

> 'Ninox Films equals 9;
> *Rescue at Sea*, the title Random House chose for my book, equals 18/9;
> The yacht's name, *Heart Light*, equals 18/9;
> *Heart Light*'s hull number equals 18/9;
> The *San Te Maru 18* equals 18/9;
> Captain Bruce White's life path equals 18/9;
> The title you chose for your doco, *South Pacific Rescue*, equals 22/4;
> David equals 22/4;
> Bruce equals 22/4;
> Storm equals 22/4;
> My life path equals 22/4.'

After explaining the significance of the numbers 18 and nine, I explained to David that the number 22/4 was known as a 'master frequency' that had to do with change on a worldwide basis. Consider what the mathematical odds might be for every 'significant' frequency surrounding this event to equal a nine and 22/4, when there are thousands of possibilities.

Statistics

Following the initial alert from *Destiny*, the New Zealand Rescue Control Centre was activated at 10:30 pm, 3 June 1994. By the time the search was suspended at 5:50 am, 8 June 1994, 22 personnel from the centre had been on duty.

The Searchers

Aircraft from the RNZAF spent 117 hours in the air. RNZAF *Monowai* searched for 98 hours; her Wasp helicopter spent 30 hours in the air.

The Rescuers

VESSELS	YACHTS FROM WHICH CREW WERE RESCUED
Jacques Cartier (French)	*Sofia* (2 people)
Nomadic Duchess (Norwegian)	*Wai Kiwi II* (5 people)
Monowai (New Zealand)	*Pilot* (2 people) *Ramtha* (2 people) *Silver Shadow* (4 people)
San Te Maru 18 (New Zealand)	*Heart Light* (4 people) (and one empty life-raft)
Tui Cakau (Fijian)	*Destiny* (2 people)
	(21 people rescued)

Missing
Quartermaster   3 people

The storm and this book are the trigger for a ripple in the consciousness of humankind. The remarkable events that have led to this book being published within three months of its completion are rare in the world of publishing, especially with the terms and conditions that had to be met. The effect that the storm has had on all who have come in contact with it emphasizes how powerful this crack in the foundation of reality is.

Do not look to your concepts to judge the reality of this event. Look deeply into your heart, your knowingness, and *feel* a deeper and greater reality. The time for understanding is at hand. This formidable opening is your opportunity to choose a new reality, a new paradigm. The answers lie *within you*.

Selling doomsday is big business. Look not to your fears, but to your hearts and the frequencies that will set you free. It has been prophesied that the teachings for 'A New Age' would come out of New Zealand. This prophesy is about to be fulfilled.

APPENDIX

A Safe Cruising Guide for Catamarans

Darryl Wheeler

While most people will not encounter hurricane conditions while cruising, it only takes one tempest to destroy life and property. Our experiences during the storm gave us an insight, not only into desirable safety precautions, but also into certain aspects of design that increased the vulnerability of our catamaran to the hazards it faced. I would like here to pass on what we learnt by offering a suggested building and safety guide.

Firstly, though, let me comment on the monohull verses multihull controversy. *Heart Light* was a 12M catamaran. *Ramtha* was a 12M catamaran. All other yachts caught up in the storm were monohulls, ranging from 11 metres to 13 metres. Most of the crews were experienced, well-seasoned cruisers.

All the monohulls that needed assistance during the

storm experienced knockdowns, being pitch-poled and/or rolled 360 degrees, with substantial damage to crew and yacht. While both cats came close to capsizing, in the end, neither did. Neither catamaran received substantial damage. Outside of bruising, no catamaran crew member suffered major injury.

Under the sea conditions experienced out there, this alone should 'put to bed' once and for all the myth about catamarans being unsafe cruising machines. After our experience, for safety reasons, we would not go back to sea in anything other than a catamaran.

Multihulls are safe. A well-built, ocean-going catamaran is as safe, if not safer, than any sea-going yacht. Both *Heart Light* and *Ramtha* proved their worth by safely getting their crew through the ultimate storm.

Now for the lessons we learnt during that tempest.

■ Autopilot ■

Here comes an endorsement for Cetrek, which turned out to be one of the most important pieces of equipment on the boat. By watching it, we were able to get a feel of what was necessary for us to do when we had to take over manually steering the boat. I was able to leave the autopilot on in all but the most extreme conditions. I was able to tweak the dial as if I was manually steering. For a while, this gave me the much-needed breaks from continually fighting the wheel. I cannot say enough for this product. We will guarantee that our next autopilot will be a Cetrek.

■ Back Door ■

We found that our back door did not have enough clearance off the cockpit sole, being only four or five inches high. It took a few moments before the drains could take away the water when a wave filled the cockpit.

So, with a back door that was not waterproof, water came in and soaked the interior carpet. Eventually, all of the carpet surface inside the boat was waterlogged. I would have an entry step of at least one foot.

■ Batteries ■

It is most important to make sure all batteries are secure. We had four six-volt batteries weighing 95 pounds each — two in the port engine room, two in the starboard engine room. After our final broach, the two batteries in the port engine-room had broken free and fell three feet on to the engine room floor. As they fell, they tore loose a lot of the wires that went to the navigation instruments and other important systems in the boat. The acid spilled out and filled the engine room with an acid-type gas. Instantly, we had a potential bomb. One spark and look out!

I had to crawl into the engine room and, with my bare hands, pick up the batteries and put them back in their holders — no easy feat in the conditions. I had to be careful not to cause a spark. Then I had to clean up the acid. My hands were burned by the acid but, luckily, no sparks were caused. Make sure all batteries are in a sealed compartment that can survive possible broaching conditions.

■ Bilge Pump ■

Every hull has to have manual bilge pumps that are easily accessible. We had electric and manual pumps, but all our manual pumps were in the floor. When the inside was trashed, we couldn't find the floor, which made it very difficult to access the manual pumps. When the batteries broke loose, we lost half of our electric bilge pumps.

It is also important that all outside compartments have manual bilge pumps. When our port stern steering compartment was breached, I had to bucket the water out of it — not much fun with waves breaking over you and pouring even more water into the compartment.

■ Cabin Locker Locks ■

You have no idea of the motion of a yacht caught up in the conditions we faced. It was like being inside a washing machine. Everything that is not secured in the inside of the boat has the potential of becoming a lethal flying missile. It is important that every cabinet have a lock on it. Everything inside our boat was trashed. Even cabinets that we thought were secure, came open. Keep in mind we did not roll or pitch-pole like some of the other yachts. I cannot imagine what the inside of their boats must have looked like.

■ Chafing ■

After our last broach, and while waiting for rescue, we put out our para-anchor. I had used my normal bridle for the drogue, which was by then securely wrapped around both props. I, therefore, deployed the para-anchor with a bridle I used when anchoring. The three-quarter-inch rope on the bridle chafed through in less than 10 hours. It had been secured to two bollards and fed through the proper deck hardware. But the violent motion of the sea just chafed it through. It is necessary to not only have stainless-steel shackles on all rope, but also the rope must be shackled on to proper deck fittings.

■ Cockpit Drains ■

We had four drain-holes that were three inches in diameter in the cockpit. While they did very well, I would almost double that size next time. Do not skimp on cockpit drains.

■ Cotter Pins ■

The cotter pin that held the nut in place on my hydraulic steering had not been checked and secured. The results could have been disastrous if the nut had fallen off. We discovered that there was only half a thread holding it on. It is important, before any sea journey, to check all cotter pins and make sure they are secure.

■ Dagger Boards ■

Although our yacht did not have dagger boards, I will comment on them. It would have been vital to pull up the dagger boards as soon as it looked like conditions were going to deteriorate. Not usually being able to pull up the boards if there is any pressure against them, means stopping the boat to raise them. The only other solution would be to have boards that would break off if the boat started to slip sideways down a wave. If you could not have raised the boards or, if they would not break off, surely you would then be in danger of tripping over them when surfing sideways, as happens during a broach. This could cause a capsize. While dagger boards are desirable going to weather, we feel our next boat will also not have them.

■ Design ■

A possible design problem we felt that we had was in our broad and flat-faced stern, around 18 feet wide and four feet high. When we were surfing down large 100-foot stacking waves that were breaking, the water would make contact with that broad surface and push us sideways. The less flat area in the stern of the boat that you present to the seas, the better you are in running.

■ Dinghy ■

Our new, hard-bottom, inflatable dinghy was securely

fastened and lashed down to the back of our catamaran. But, in spite of all of our precautions, it still broke free and threatened to punch a hole in the boat. If at all possible, we would recommend stowing an inflatable dinghy below deck. Anything that is on deck could and will be swept off in the type of conditions we experienced.

■ Drogues ■

We deployed a six-foot diameter chute with 50 feet of chain attached to 75 feet of rope hooked to a 100-foot bridle. The chute was made of nylon and was attached to the chain with a swivel. The wind had reached 50 knots and the seas had built to about 40 feet. After the drogue was deployed, the autopilot had a much easier time controlling the boat.

The key was the bridle, which was shackled on the end of each hull. Note here that it is imperative to use metal shackles and have metal eyelets in the rope to prevent chafing through of the rope. As the boat would try to veer off while surfing down the huge seas, the drogue would help pull her stern back. This meant we surfed directly down the seas. The drogue was one of the most important parts of our survival gear.

■ EPIRB ■

I would have to say that an EPIRB is the single most important piece of equipment on a boat. The Orions found us soon after we set ours off. Without it, there may be very little hope of being found. It is hard enough to spot a boat from the air in perfect conditions, let alone in the conditions we were in, where visibility was very, very poor.

■ Exhaust Systems ■

Both of our engines had exhaust systems that exited out of the stern of the boat. Both systems had a large loop in the tubing. In the end, both engines were totally ruined by sea water and were inoperable. This happened to several other boats, including monohulls with rear exhaust pipes. The force of the waves drove the water up through the exhaust and into the engines. On our next boat, we will try to have the exhaust exit on the side.

■ Inside Steering ■

We had two helm stations — one outside, the other inside. We helmed the boat from the inside. None of us would have wanted to be outside in those conditions. I do not think I could have sat on the helm as long as I did had I been outside. Rain and spray being driven horizontally by 90-knot winds would have made life too miserable in the open cockpit, assuming I wasn't bashed to death or washed overboard in the meantime. An inside steering station is vital for ocean-going cruisers.

■ Instruments ■

All of our navigational and communication instruments were inside the boat, where we thought they were safe from the elements. On our last broach, a huge wave poured water into the interior, thereby shorting out my SSB radio. This effectively cut off all communication from the outside world. I could not get weather reports or let anyone know we were alive and give our coordinates.

After losing our main VHF due to dead batteries, we had a hand-held VHF radio that I had charged before we left port. This became our life-line, the only way we could communicate to the Orion planes and the rescue vessel. A hand-held VHF is an absolute must as a back-up system.

In the future, I will have a waterproof cover over our communications equipment. Without communication, you could be lost. It is vital to protect your link to the outside world.

■ Lashing ■

It is important to keep some sort of lashing material next to the helm station. After our final broach, we were helpless. All the engines were out, the props were wrapped in the drogue and rope, and we were lying a hull to huge seas. As the waves came, the bow would fall off and we would start to accelerate out of control down the face of the wave. We quickly lashed the steering wheel hard to starboard. Then, as the boat would start down the face of the wave, she would round up and lie sideways to the seas. This was much safer than racing off out of control down the face of the monsters we faced. You do not have time to look around for a lashing, so have one handy.

■ Life-rafts ■

There was no way anyone could get into a life-raft in the type of conditions the storm presented. The size of the waves, the wind and the motion of the boat all precluded that. A life-raft should be tried only as a last resort, when your boat is getting ready to sink to the bottom of the sea.

■ Locker Hatches ■

We had a large number of lockers, almost all of which were filled with water despite very secure hatches. One locker came open. It is very important to make sure that all deck hatches can be locked down, and everything in the lockers secured. Ideally, the hatches should be waterproof. A lot of weight can be taken on when lockers fill with water.

Securing the anchor is especially important. Many cruisers stow their anchors in a hatch without securing them. Imagine a 50-pound hunk of metal, that has the potential to become a battering ram, banging around! Not a pleasant possibility.

■ Para-anchors ■

We had an 18-foot diameter para-anchor with 600 feet of rope and a 150-foot bridle. As the seas built, we had to chose either to run with the waves or deploy the para-anchor and ride it out. We feel that our decision to run with the storm was the right one since the waves, at times, were over 100 feet. As 40 to 50 feet seas stacked up on top of each other, three high, the middle wave would drop out, sending thousands of gallons of water crashing down into the trough below. Tethered to a para-anchor bow first into the waves, we would surely not have survived. The force and weight of the water would have punched out the windows and filled *Heart Light* with water. While I believe that a para-anchor is a necessary part of offshore inventory, I feel it would have been suicide to deploy it in the conditions we encountered.

■ Propellers ■

We had both engines running during the storm. When we started surfing down the mammoth waves, we would have to simultaneously turn the wheel and jam open the throttle of one of the engines to prevent broaching. Unfortunately, we broached three times. The third time, the wave carried forward all of the rope from our drogue, and both propellers and shafts became totally entangled. This may have been the reason for the crack in our hull.

The rope was wrapped so solidly that you could have played a tune on the rope tension between the two hulls. The only possible preventative measure here would have been rope cutters on the propellers. But, even then, would those cutters have been able to sever the three-quarter inch rope?

■ Safety Harnesses ■

Just as it is important to wear safety harnesses, it is equally important to have adequate places on which to clip them. We found we sorely lacked clip-on places in our cockpit, mainly because we had never visualized a need to clip on when in there. But when Shane had to go out to finally cut the dinghy free, he had nothing to clip on to in a cockpit that was six feet by nine feet.

■ Sail Sheets ■

We had a boom-roller furling system on our mainsail. It was a great system, apart from the fact that, on both sides of the mast, we had to have halyards on which to run up our flags. During the storm, these halyards became so entangled with the mainsail halyard that it was impossible to raise our mainsail. And, naturally, it was impossible to go up the mast to try to unwind the mess. Should we sail into other storms in the future, we will be making sure that all unnecessary halyards, lines, etc are taken down so that nothing can tangle up the mainsail halyard.

■ Underwater Repair ■

We used underwater epoxy to seal a crack in our hull after bailing out the compartment. At first, we mixed the epoxy and slapped it on to the crack. However, as the seawater poured in, it just washed away the epoxy. After bailing out again, we applied epoxy to the back of a piece of linoleum and placed the linoleum over the hole, weighing it down with the dinghy anchor. That did the job. The lesson learned here is to have a lot of epoxy and something like linoleum ready to seal any breaches in the hull.

■ Vents ■

Just before sailing, we had installed two new solar-powered vents over the staterooms, on the top of the boat. These proved to be a real problem. Whenever a wave engulfed us, gallons of water would pour through these vents, soaking the beds. The end result was no dry place on which to lie down. Whatever type of vent you install, make sure it is guaranteed waterproof.

■ Windows ■

Being a catamaran, *Heart Light* had many glass windows. These proved to be the most vulnerable part of the boat. When waves crashed against the windows, the frames would flex inward, allowing gallons of water to pour in. Our storm coverings across all the front windows were ripped off during the height of the storm. No matter how tempting wide seascapes are, we recommend keeping the number of windows to a minimum. At the very least, have properly designed storm coverings that cannot be ripped off by the tremendous force of the seas. The expanse of glass on *Heart Light* contributed to our decision not to para-anchor bow first into the onslaught.

In closing, we hope that others can benefit from our experience. We also hope and pray that no one else will ever be caught out in a storm like the one we endured. Ignorance may be bliss, but on the high seas it can be deadly!

Epilogue

Contained within the pages of this book, for the serious seeker, is the truth of what is taking place in the whole of the third dimension. The global shift that the world has been waiting for has begun. It is not taking place in the way human consciousness predicted, and needs to be understood in order to embrace the new reality that is being birthed. This book was written on three levels of understanding: the physical, the mental, and the spiritual. It must be studied through these different filters to find the whole of the truth contained within and between the lines.

Following this work will be a series called the *Brahman Legacy* (BRIH). In this series, you will find the complete knowledge that was given in the vortex for those souls specifically interested in the New Paradigm of the Seventh Realm.

■ Personal Enquiries ■

If you wish to write to Diviana, please give your full address, including city, state, country and zip code, as necessary. *Please also enclose a self-addressed stamped envelope.* Mail to: Diviana Illumin Brahman, PO Box 36-574, Northcote, Auckland, New Zealand.